MANAGEMENT

PHYSICS

A Common-Sense Guide to Management

2nd Edition

By Jerry Mar

ISBN 9798686349049

Preface

An ideal book for new and novice managers. 100+ figures and diagrams are used to provide a broad overview of management in a short, easy-to-read book.

In contrast to books relying on case studies, this book uses common-sense logic to explain established management concepts. This approach will especially appeal to managers in scientific and engineering fields, ones familiar with reasoning around "fundamental principles" and "laws". This book provides a parallel in the management world, by describing 30+ concepts that can help managers make common-sense, logic-based decisions - ones that will maximize chances of success.

Having sufficient information is key to making good decisions. As a result, approximately half the book is devoted to this purpose. Topics discussed include information mining, information turns, learning curves, resource cliffs, collective problem solving, one-on-one meetings, metrics, technology drivers, disruptive technologies, models, role of visionaries, and long-range planning.

There will always be unknowns, however, so management results can never be guaranteed. So, the other half of the book is devoted to maximizing chances of success. Topics here include working with uncertainty, time-resource optimization, critical path identification, management leverage, multitasking, root-cause analysis, modularization, balancing rewards and risks, model-based optimization, business planning, and managing change.

Collectively, the concepts covered provide managers with the toolbox and insight for developing common-sense, logic-based solutions for their unique problems.

The book represents the wisdom the author has gained through 34 years of management practice, coupled with observations of some of the best managers in the industry.

Acknowledgements

I would like to thank the many managers and colleagues that I have had the privilege of working with and learning from in my professional career. I have observed truly exceptional managers – some with amazing abilities to lead, motivate, and inspire. I will not list their names as there are many, and I do not wish to omit anyone by accident.

I have learned successful managers are a diverse lot – and not ones that can be typified by a single set of attributes or management style. Every business situation is unique and has its own set of management challenges. Accelerating changes in technology and the global economy promise this will be even truer in the future. The best managers are flexible, know their capabilities, and know when to seek help.

I would also like to thank my family – my wife, Linda, and my son and daughter, David and Lisa, for their unwavering encouragement during the writing of this book. I would also like to thank them for valuable suggestions during proofreading of the manuscript.

About the Author

Jerry Mar has more than 34 years of experience in management. This includes managerial roles in product engineering, technology development, and software development. He participated in the early silicon chip development at Bell Laboratories and Intel Corporation, work for which he was awarded ten U.S. patents.

At Intel he led early development of electrically-erasable (Flash) nonvolatile memory technologies. He also pioneered the development of physics-based computer-aided design tools for microchip products and chip manufacturing - building an industry-leading Technology Computer Aided Design organization in the process (one he directed for more than ten years). Jerry also ran an independent consulting company for two years to help clients apply microchip technologies to their problems. Lastly, Jerry Mar served as a volunteer management consultant with the Silicon Valley chapter of the nonprofit organization SCORE (Service Core of Retired Executives) for more than ten years, where he provided guidance to small business startups and existing businesses. Jerry is also the author of two early books on the use of personal computers. He also worked as a newspaper political cartoonist and commercial artist during his high school years in his hometown, Port Alberni, in Canada.

Jerry Mar holds B.S. and Ph.D. degrees in physics from the University of British Columbia in Canada, and the California Institute of Technology in Pasadena, California, respectively.

Table of Contents

1. Introduction

This book is all about *common-sense management*. It will show how analysis and common-sense logic can help managers do a better job.

Imagine two managers facing a problem. One manager analyzes available information about the problem and resources for tackling it, then methodically formulates the best approach for solving the problem. The other manager looks at the problem and uses intuition to quickly select a solution approach. It should not be a surprise that managers in the first category are routinely more successful than those in the second. The difference is the first manager is driven by logic while the second manager is driven by emotion.

Despite this fact, many managers find it hard to apply common sense to management problems. In my professional career - both as a manager in technology companies and an independent business consultant - I have been surprised to see intelligent, highly educated people making seemingly illogical decisions. At times, it appeared their decisions contradicted obvious facts and were driven by imaginary forces. Not surprising, such decisions rarely led to business success. What I found puzzling was how intelligent people could be so illogical in their actions.

"But getting to B is shorter using this path."
"No, I always take this path when I go to B."

Figure 1.1 People prefer the familiar versus logic to guide their actions.

Let me give you an example of illogical business thinking. Suppose progress at the two-thirds point in a project is well behind plan. Managers who believe plan objectives can still be met without changing existing processes are not thinking logically. For that to happen, the rate of progress would have to be *faster* than plan for the remaining third of the project (see Fig. 1.2).

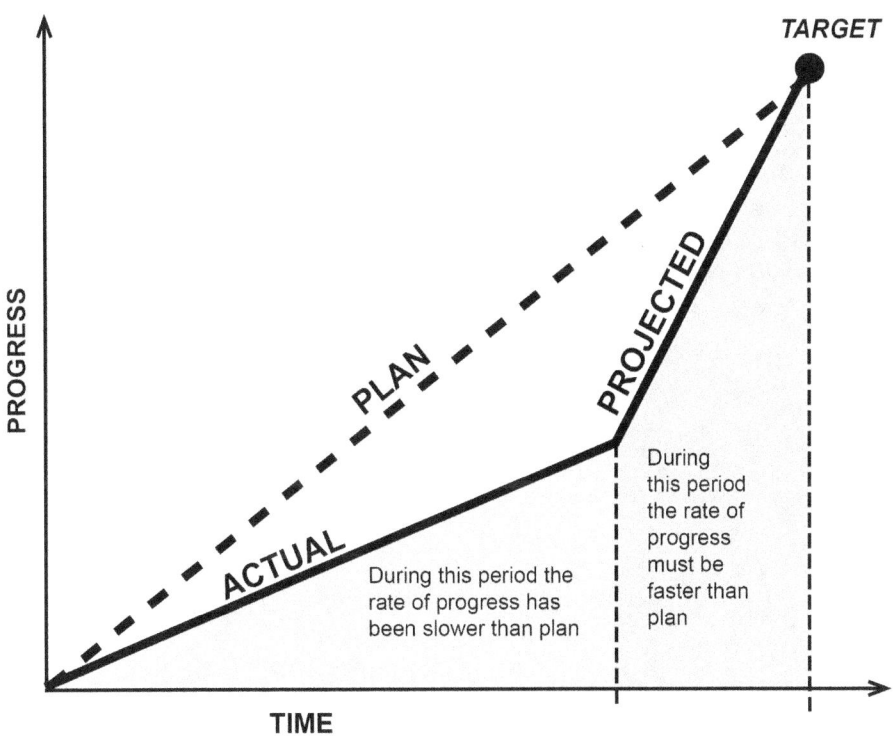

Figure 1.2   This graph shows why "catching up to plan" when one is behind is difficult if processes are unchanged.

This is highly unlikely if there are no changes to people, resources, or processes. Projects rarely fall behind simply because workers are "lazy" and "need to work harder". More often they fall behind because of unforeseen difficulties. Without process changes, progress is likely to continue at the same rate - namely slower than plan - resulting in project targets not met. Managers who feel schedules can be made up by simply having everyone work harder are often not facing up to underlying problems.

In the above example, the illogic thinking is assuming the same actions will produce different results. Another example along these same lines is when a person repeats unconvincing arguments. Unless the audience has hearing difficulties, if they were not convinced the first time, it is unlikely they will be convinced on hearing the arguments repeated. The audience may cease arguing after it tires of hearing the same arguments, but exhaustion is not the same as agreement.

Another example of illogical business thinking is when short-term pressures drive decisions without regard to the larger picture. How often have we heard the refrain "I can't deal with anything else right now, I'm overloaded with work that needs to be completed today"? Stressed managers whose only goal is to make it through the day are in this group. For them, immediate pressures (real or imagined) are driving actions – not reasoning. This can cause managers to miss looming problems, which can result in worse situations in the future.

We really need to get this roof fixed,
it always leaks in storms ...

Figure 1.3 Focusing on the immediate and ignoring the bigger picture
can be hazardous.

Charisma and Common-Sense Management

People admire charismatic leaders. These are leaders who are extraordinary skilled in communicating and promoting their views. Such leaders have an advantage, as many people will follow their guidance strictly on faith. Charisma, unfortunately, doesn't help pick the right direction. In fact, charisma may make it more difficult to select the right direction, as others may blindly trust the leader and not contribute their own thinking. In short, common-sense decision making is still crucial – charismatic leaders simply facilitate their execution.

Common-sense management means collecting as much information as possible about a problem and analyzing it to determine the best course of action. Management leadership is more than just leading; it is also about leading in the right direction (see Fig. 1.4).

"Follow me, team, I'm sure this is the right direction..."

Figure 1.4 Management leadership means leading in the right direction.

Picking the right direction requires objective analyses of available options and selecting the best approach. The process for doing this is data collection and logical analysis. There are many different ways of solving any problem, with the number of ways increasing with the complexity of the problem. Selecting among the myriad of possible solution paths is one of the challenges of management.

By objectively analyzing available information one can determine which solution options are most promising. Although each option has uncertainties, some options are more likely to succeed than others. Analyses can be used to rule out those least likely to succeed and make planning tractable.

Decisions based on logical analyses have other benefits. Such decisions are perceived as more objective than those based on intuition or "gut feel". Opinion surveys routinely show employees rank fairness and integrity among the most desired attributes in their leaders. A culture in which objective reasoning is prized is one that promotes objectivity and teamwork over politics.

Why Common-Sense Management Is Difficult

Common sense management is not practiced as broadly as it could because many find it difficult to apply "logical analysis" to management situations. The unpredictability of human behavior, the complexity of business environments, and the lack of detailed information about external influences, make it difficult to predict precise outcomes from any management action. This is illustrated in Fig. 1.5, which compares actual project execution against planned execution.

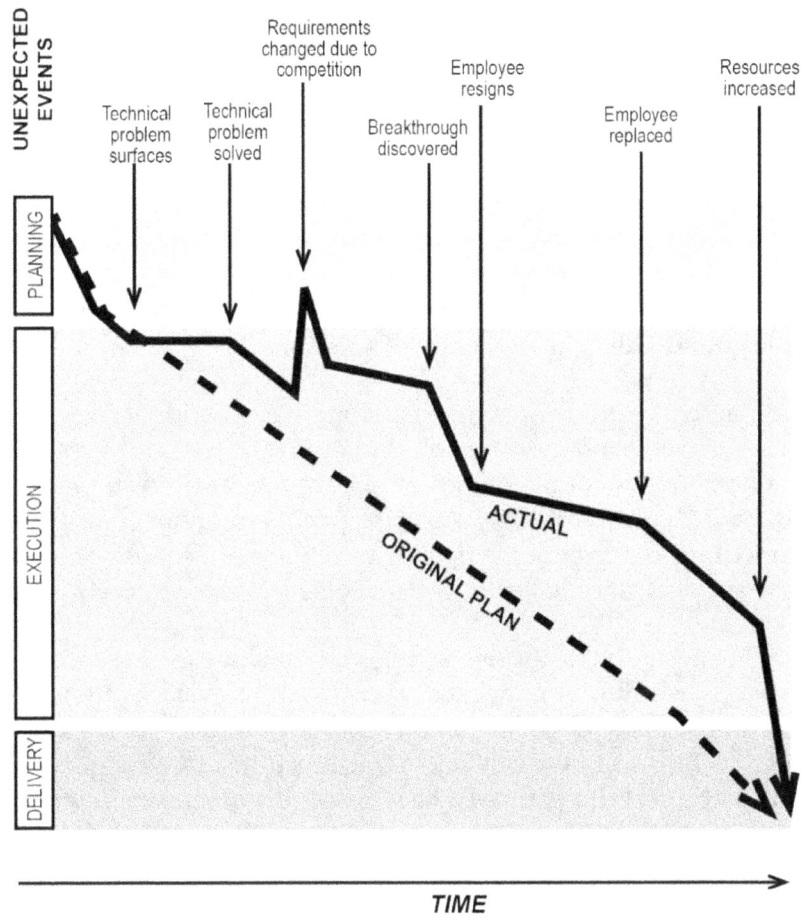

Figure 1.5 How unexpected events can influence plans.

The uncertainty inherent in any management action makes it difficult to determine optimum courses of action. As a result, some managers feel logical analysis is of limited value in management and rely more on experience and intuition to guide their decision-making.

Unfortunately, while intuition, "gut feel", or "seat of the pants" decision-making has value, they are ineffective tools for day-to-day decision-making. Over-reliance on them can lead to reactive, aimless leadership. It means being guided more by one's emotions, emotions that are oftentimes determined by factors outside of the business problem.   For example, *personal biases* (prejudices about specific approaches, people, ...) can cause such decision makers to exclude superior courses of action.   Likewise, *comfort* (similarity of the approach to past projects) may cause decision makers to choose more familiar but less optimal solutions.   *Political pressures* (imagined views of superiors, peers, or subordinates) can also cause decision makers to unnecessarily limit options. Even one's *personal mood* (how well a person slept, whether he or she argued with their spouse, ...) can influence the "gut" selection of solutions.

Emotions and passion are important, but they should *complement*, not replace objective analyses of solution options. While it is true there are uncertainties in all courses of action (e.g., a perfectly executed plan could be thwarted by surprise product announcements by a competitor), it does not mean all action plans are equal. There is in fact a *best* plan, and that is the *plan with the greatest likelihood of success.*

Managers, especially those starting new businesses, are faced with an overwhelming number of decisions.   Novice entrepreneurs sometimes throw up their hands and jump in and pick a random direction to begin new businesses. Unfortunately, doing so rarely leads to the best direction. To be successful, new businesses need to take business from competitors. Even the second-best approach might not be adequate if competitors are utilizing the best approach.

The challenge is how to use available information to find the best solutions. That is the purpose of this book.

What Is In This Book

This book introduces common-sense management concepts and rules of thumb that can be applied to a wide range of management situations. It shows how they can be used to build a framework for logical analysis. The basic management concepts introduced in this book are somewhat analogous to physical laws in science - hence the title of this book: "Management Physics". When used appropriately, these management concepts can serve as building blocks for analyzing management problems and finding optimum solutions. Such analyses can be used to narrow the solution space by eliminating options less likely to succeed. They can also be used to identify courses of action with the best chances of success. This frees up management judgment to focus on areas where most needed – areas with insufficient data.

One might think it ridiculous to apply "physics-like" reasoning to the fuzzy world of management, since reasoning in physical sciences is built on deductive reasoning around precise physical laws – laws for which there are no counterparts in management. In fact, the physics of matter is actually "fuzzy" at subatomic dimensions. At those dimensions, it is not possible to precisely specify the position or energy of basic particles of matter at any given moment of time. The mathematical formulation of physics at subatomic dimensions (quantum physics) describes only the probabilities of particles being in certain states – not where the particles actually are. It is the statistical averaging of many particle states that gives stable predictable states for the large objects that people routinely encounter (like rocks, trees, and other people), as they are made up of multi-trillions of atoms and smaller particles where the fuzziness of the subatomic behavior has been averaged out.

An analogous situation exists in management. Although all actions have uncertainties, there are still trends that are meaningful when the uncertainties are averaged out. This means it is still possible to apply reasoning to determine which directions are most likely to succeed given available information. And although the uncertainties may cause some of those directions to be wrong, applying such reasoning results in correct solutions more often. Being correct more than your competitors is a winning business strategy.

The book starts with a chapter on basic definitions and fundamental concepts. Additional concepts are introduced in subsequent chapters, grouped by application theme. Their use in real-life management situations is illustrated with examples. The chapters are best read in order, as later topics utilize concepts introduced in earlier chapters. Diagrams, figures, and pictures are used liberally to make the concepts as clear as possible.

Who Is This Book For?

This book is for all people managers, but especially beginning managers. Although the concepts in this book are applicable to all levels of management – from beginning supervisors to senior managers leading large organizations – it is most useful to those developing their management skills and styles. It can also be useful for people assisting managers, especially those formulating plans and strategies.

Summary

As stated earlier, the common-sense concepts described in this book are meant to supplement, not replace intuition and passion. Their purpose is to enable managers to take maximum advantage of available information when making decisions. In many ways, logical analysis is the easy part of management, as these are tasks that can be performed mechanically. It makes sense that managers should use such techniques to the maximum extent possible.

Logical analysis frees up managers' time, so they can focus their intuitive skills where most needed – in areas with insufficient information. In my experience, the best managers leverage logical reasoning to the fullest - and use it to multiply other strengths like vision, drive, and leadership.

The combination of data collection, logical analysis, and reasoned judgment is the essence of *common-sense management*.

2. The Management Job

In order to apply logical concepts to management, we need to first agree on what the "job of management" is. Is it defining company business strategies? Is it determining how finances and resources are allocated? Is it generating staffing plans and hiring employees? Is it selling business plans to investors to obtain financing? Is it developing marketing and sales programs for the company? Is it supervising employees in their work? Is it directing teams for solving specific problems and tasks? The answer: it is all of these.

All of these jobs have two common attributes. They all have specific *objectives* and they all require *resources* to achieve those objectives. I will use the term "project" to represent this gamut of jobs. This is a broader definition of "projects" than is common, as "project management" traditionally refers to the management of small groups of people solving specific problems and tasks. Our broader definition of projects includes all jobs that utilize resources to achieve objectives. Using this broader definition, the job of management is *orchestrating the application of resources to achieve project objectives.* Basically, it is managing a system made up of the following components:

1. **OBJECTIVES:** Objectives that the manager and his or her organization has targeted, with specific goals and times they are to be achieved.

2. **RESOURCES:** People, equipment, tools, facilities, intellectual property, vendors, money, etc., that the manager has at his or her disposal for achieving objectives.

3. **PLAN:** Plan of action for using available resources to achieve objectives.

4. **EXECUTION:** Execution of the plan.

The flow diagram in Fig. 2.1 depicts such a system. The solid downward arrows denote the normal direction of management information flow in a project. First objectives are set, resources allocated, plan defined, and plan executed. The diagram also shows dashed upward arrows. The dashed ones from plan back up to resources and objectives recognize resources or objectives may need to be adjusted to come up with a suitable plan. The dashed one from execution up to plan recognizes plans may also need adjustment if unexpected problems arise during execution.

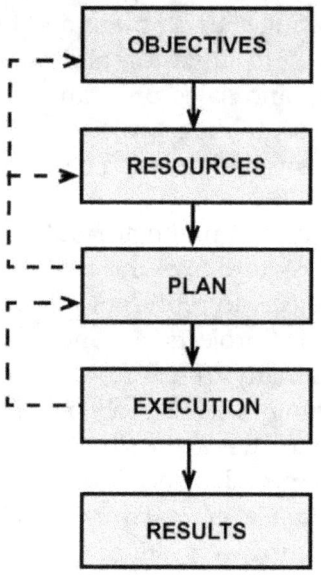

Figure 2.1 Basic elements of a project

Using our broader definition of projects, project sizes can differ widely depending on the level of responsibility of the manager. It should be noted that in our definition, the selection and definition of a project is itself a project, just one at a higher level.

Large projects tend to spawn many smaller subprojects, each managed by lower-level managers. Likewise, there could be subprojects within those subprojects, each focusing on an increasingly narrow part of the larger project. An example two-level project hierarchy is depicted in the Fig. 2.2 below.

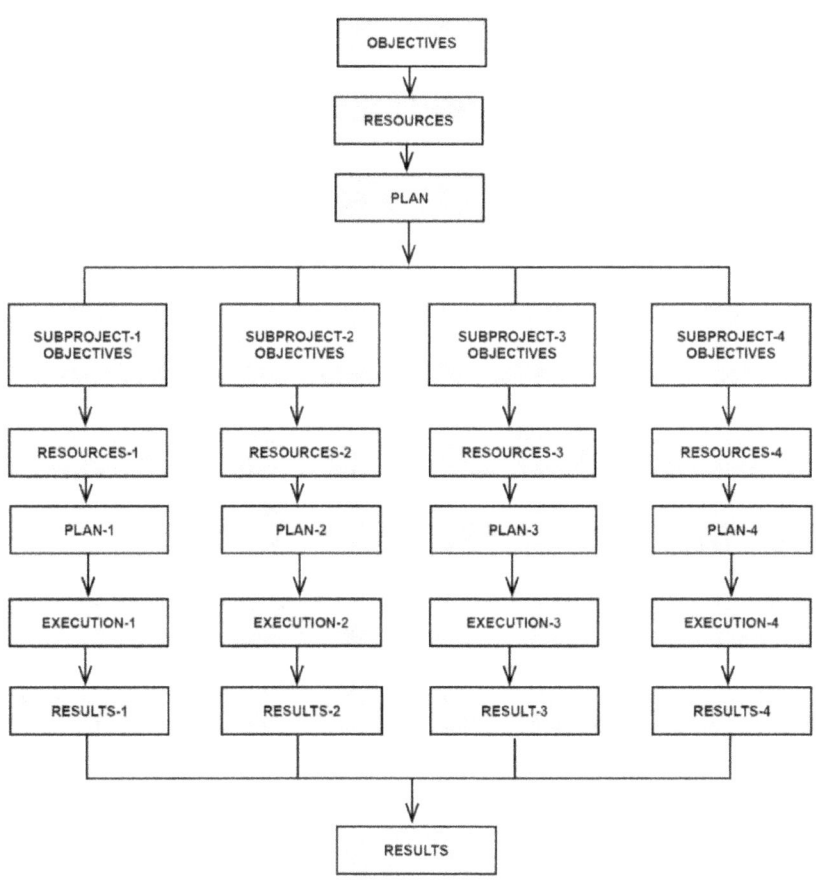

Figure 2.2 Example of a hierarchy of projects

In each case the highest-level project provides the framework for objectives and planning in the lower-level projects, with execution taking place at the lowest level projects. For example, a higher-level project might be moving a new product into manufacturing. This in turn could include subprojects for expanding manufacturing capacity, optimizing equipment utilization, and improving manufacturing yield - all of which are parts of the higher-level project.

Every project has a *beginning* (objectives) and an *end* (results). Projects end as *successes* when objectives are achieved, or as *failures* when they are not. The manager's job is to orchestrate activities in a project to make it successful. In large projects this includes ensuring managers of subprojects understand how their objectives tie into larger project goals. Subproject managers can sometimes get overly engrossed in operational details and lose sight of the objectives of the larger project. The job of management is more than supervising people doing their jobs; it also includes ensuring the *right jobs* are done (see Fig. 2.3).

Figure 2.3 It is important that the right job be done.

Tactical versus Strategic Planning

From the preceding, it should be clear that planning is an essential part of the management job. Planning can be categorized as either *tactical* or *strategic*.

Tactical plans define specific actions for achieving, specific near-term goals. An example would be plans for decreasing the manufacturing cost of a product. Tactical plans might include negotiating with vendors to lower component prices, increasing the utilization of key manufacturing equipment, or training employees to improve screening of defects. Each of these tactical plans define specific actions that can be taken to contribute to the near-term goal: decreasing the manufacturing cost of the product.

Strategic plans, on the other hand, address general approaches for tackling a business area over the longer term. For example, a technology company specializing in high-end products might decide to broaden its market by adding low and mid-range products in order to broaden its markets and strengthen its purchasing position for components. Notice this strategy defines a general approach – not specific near-term actions. Tactical plans aligned with this strategy are needed to execute the strategy.

Uncertainty and the Job of Management

Earlier we stated the manager's job is "orchestrating activities in a project to successfully achieve project objectives". Since these are activities of people, orchestration means steering human behavior of subordinates, co-workers, vendors, customers, etc. Experienced managers know this is not an easy task, as people are not machines, but somewhat unpredictable emotional animals whose behaviors are influenced by variables outside the manager's control. Problems at home, how well the person slept, relations with co-workers, personal ambitions, prior experiences - all can affect people behavior. Events external to the project (e.g., competition, technology advances, market shifts, etc.) can also affect outcomes.

Managers have limited visibility into many of these variables and cannot precisely predict what will happen when executing plans. This means there is uncertainty in every plan. For example, there are *uncertainties in objectives* (e.g., goals may be inadequate if competitors introduce superior products or market demand shifts). There is also *uncertainty in resources* (e.g., key employees may resign, vendors may not meet delivery commitments, unexpected business conditions may force reductions in budgets, etc.). And there is always *uncertainty in execution* (e.g., unanticipated technical problems, equipment failures, employee illness, etc.).

Such uncertainties might cause one to conclude detailed planning is futile - that managers should focus their efforts on honing skills for reacting to unforeseen events. Nothing could be further from the truth. Uncertainty does not mean all courses of management action are equal - only that all courses of action have uncertainties. Uncertainty means more scenarios need to be considered, namely *more planning not less*. Consequently, our definition of the job of management needs to be refined as follows:

The job of management is orchestrating activities to maximize the probability of achieving project objectives

This definition acknowledges that the consequences of management actions are always uncertain. The best any manager can do is to select actions that maximize the likelihood of success. While some may feel this is too weak an objective and that success must be the imperative - edicts cannot change reality. Maximizing the probability of success is in fact *the best that can be done*. Furthermore, such a strategy is consistent with being successful over the long term. An organization that routinely maximizes the likelihood of success will have more successes than its competitors and more likely to become the leader.

Just as nothing is certain in life, uncertainty in management decisions is a fact of life. Although we can strive to be secure in our lives, we are still prey to accidents, illnesses, criminal acts, wars, earthquakes, and storms. The best we can do is to pick actions that reduce the likelihood of such events and minimize their consequences when they occur.

Our *probabilistic definition of the job of management* has broad implications. Indirect activities that are not part of the primary project need to be considered. For example, programs that build employee skills, enhance communication, raise morale, and foster partnerships produce stronger and stabler work environments - ones better able to handle surprises and uncertainties. Maximizing the probability of success also requires managers to examine multiple business scenarios to ensure the most promising approach is selected and to have backup approaches if the selected approach runs into problems. In short, the job of management requires allocating resources for both direct and indirect activities in order to maximize the probability that project objectives will be achieved.

Summary

The overall job of management is orchestrating the utilization of resources to achieve specific business objectives. Planning is an essential part of every manager's job. When planning is focused on the immediate actions for achieving near-term goals they are referred to as tactical. In contrast, plans that define general approaches for achieving longer-range objectives are referred to as strategic.

In the world of management, all actions have uncertainties. Consequently, the job of management is orchestrating activities to maximize the probability of successfully achieving project objectives.

Doing so requires examining different approaches for achieving objectives and picking ones with the greatest chance of success, as well as identifying contingency plans for unexpected problems. It also includes fostering work environments that are better at handling uncertainty.

Planning is an essential part of the job of management. Fig. 2.4 depicts the basic planning process: problem definition, information collection, solutions development, and solution selection.

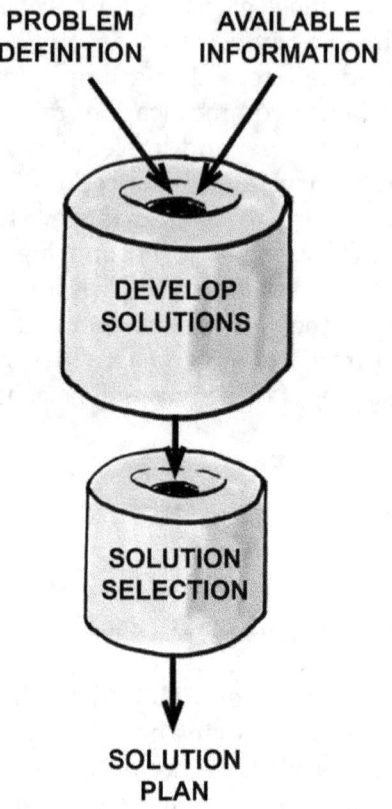

Figure 2.4 Basic planning process.

3. Working with Uncertainty

The fact that there is uncertainty in all management actions needs to be incorporated into management reasoning. Words like "will" and "cause" need to be replaced by "probably will" and "likely cause". In short, while we cannot say with certainty what *will* happen, we can say what *will most likely* happen. While this difference may appear to be merely semantics, the implications are far more profound. The latter implies a broader range of scenarios, including: "what is second most likely to happen", "what is third most likely to happen", etc. Thus, we must learn to deal with multiple scenarios and their *probabilities* (likelihood of happening).

A manager's job has been likened to that of a juggler trying to keep many balls in midair at the same time. In the probabilistic view of management, it is like a juggler keeping a bunch of *fuzzy* balls in the air at the same time (see Fig 3.1). Although the manager does not know the precise location of any given ball, he or she can still juggle using the most likely position of each ball. Doing do will lead to the fewest balls dropped and the best juggling job possible. In business, this means doing the best job possible - more important, a better job than competitors.

Figure 3.1 Managers juggle many fuzzy balls at the same time.

So how does one determine which project plan has the best chance of succeeding? The answer is surprisingly simple. Rational managers will only put together project plans that will be successful if everything goes as intended (i.e., rational managers will not devise project plans designed to fail). Consequently, the likelihood of *failure* of any rational plan depends on the likelihood of that plan *not behaving as planned.* The probability of this occurring is directly dependent on the uncertainty in the plan. More uncertainty means more chances for plan failure. Conversely, the plan with the least amount of uncertainty is the one most likely to behave as planned. This notion can be summarized as follows:

The project plan with the greatest chance of success is the one with the least amount of uncertainty

But you ask, can't uncertainty also be positive? Couldn't plans turn out *better* than expected - finish earlier than planned and utilize fewer resources? While this can happen, positive uncertainties do not change the desired outcomes of plans – they are successful whether they turn out as planned or better. Therefore we need only be concerned with the negative uncertainties, as they are the only ones that can derail plans. Usually, the negative uncertainties are also much greater than the positive uncertainties.

When evaluating uncertainties in a project it is important that the uncertainties of all parts of the project be included. For example, an action plan with modest goals might have low *execution* uncertainty, but that same plan might have high *goal* uncertainty if the targets are too modest (i.e., the goals may result in products that are not competitive). Assessing overall risk is an area where logic and human judgment converge. Logical analyses can identify uncertainties, but weighing and gauging risk requires management judgment.

The experience of the manager and organization is a major factor affecting uncertainty. For example, an experienced computer chip design manager is more likely to pick better actions for designing the next computer chip than a person who has only managed production testing. In general, execution uncertainties are lower if planned actions are similar to those in previous successful projects, namely:

Uncertainties are lower when projects are similar to previously successful projects

The corollary to this concept is project uncertainty increases the more a project differs from previous projects. For example, the further into the future a project's objectives, the greater project uncertainty - since past experiences are less relevant and unanticipated events are more likely (e.g., unforeseen competition, technological breakthroughs, market shifts, etc.).

Project uncertainties increase the further into the future target objectives

In summary, the more we move into areas where we have little experience - whether due to unfamiliar fields or unfamiliar time (e.g., distant future) - the poorer our visibility and greater the risk we will take wrong actions.

Figure 3.2 We have a clearer view of where we have been than where we are going.

The exception to this rule is when project goals are very modest. In such cases, risks are low at the start and moving the goal further into the future simply provides more time to accomplish the same goals. This situation is the exception in the competitive world of business.

Numerical Specification of Probability

At this point it is worthwhile spending some time on the numerical specification of probability. Probabilities are typically specified by a decimal number between 0 and 1, where 0 means 0% chance of happening, 0.3 means 30% chance of happening, and 1 means 100% chance of happening. Using this scale, there is a simple relationship between probability of success and probability of failure - since they are complements of each another. The probability of success is simply 1.0 minus the probability of failure. For example, if the probability of failure is 0.2 or 20%, the probability of success must be 1 - 0.2 = 0.8 or 80%. The same relationship can also be used to translate in the other direction - namely, the probability of failure is 1.0 minus the probability of success.

But how does one determine the probability of success for a specific action? How does one decide if it is 45% or 50%? This is where management judgment plays a role. Experience with past projects, knowledge of resources (e.g., staffing, infrastructure and marketing strengths), plus understanding of the relative difficulty of planned actions, can be combined to estimate the likelihood of success. In some cases, the best guess may simply confine the probability of success to broad ranges. For example, the numbers 25%, 50% or 80% might represent low chance, even chance, or high chance of success. In such cases the difference between 55% versus 50% is not meaningful. In situations where significant data exists from similar projects, more precise probability numbers can be estimated for planned actions.

For projects, the probability of project success is the *product* of the probabilities that project goals are competitive and project execution is successful; since *both* must be successful to meet business objectives (resource risk is incorporated in execution risk). For example, if the probability of the goals being competitive is 60% and the probability of successful execution is 80%, the overall probability of success will be 0.6 x 0.8 = 0.48, or approximately 50%.

This multiplication of probabilities of success of individual activities to estimate the overall probability of success is valid whenever activities are ones that *must* be successful for the overall project to succeed. Such activities are called **critical path** activities. This is illustrated in the Fig. 3.3. The person at A will reach his destination, B, only if she can successfully pull herself up the rope, cross the bridge, and climb the ladder - each of these activities are critical paths to getting from A to B.

Figure 3.3 The person will make it from A to B only if she successfully climbs the rope, crosses the bridge, and climbs the ladder.

The critical path steps above are represented in the simple flow diagram in Fig. 3.4 below.

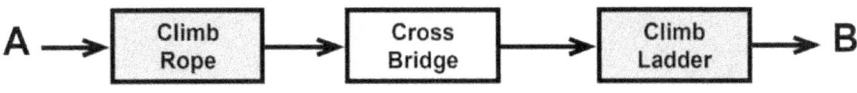

Figure 3.4 Flow diagram representation of the critical paths in Fig. 3.3

Combining Probabilities

The basis for combining probabilities is easier to understand if one views probabilities as the percentage of successes in a large number of attempts. In the example in Fig 3.3 suppose the success probabilities of climbing the rope, crossing the bridge, and climbing the ladder are 0.6, 0.8, and 0.9, respectively. This means if a hundred people attempt to go from A to B, only 60 will successfully climb the rope. Of those 60 only 60 x 0.8 = 48 will make it across the bridge, and of those 48 only 48 x 0.9 = 43 will reach the top of the ladder. Thus, the overall probability of success is 43%, which is 0.6 x 0.8 x 0.9.

Notice that the overall probability of success is always less than the probability of success of any of its constituent critical paths, namely:

The probability of success of a project is always lower than the probability of success of any of its critical paths

Increasing the probability of success of a project requires increasing the probability of success of its critical paths. Not all critical path improvements contribute the same, however. The overall increase will be greatest when we raise the probability of success of the lowest probability critical path. For example, if in our previous example we were to raise the success probability for the rope climbing step by 10% from 0.6 to 0.7, the overall success probability would increase to 0.7 x 0.8 x 0.9 = 0.50 (50%), a 7% increase. On the other hand, had we instead raised the success probability of the ladder climbing step by 10% from 0.9 to 1.0, the overall probability of success would be 0.6 x 0.8 x 1.0 = 0.48 (48%), only a 5% increase. In general:

The probability of project success increases more when we increase the success probabilities of high-risk versus low-risk critical paths

This rule can conflict with human nature. Managers, like all humans, like to focus their energies on what they do well (namely the lower risk critical paths), since they know what to do and are confident of the results. It takes courage to direct resources to unfamiliar areas (the riskier critical paths) - yet those are precisely the areas that will contribute most to improving the chances of success of the overall project. For example, it would take infinite resources to increase the success probability of a strong critical path from 99% to 100% (the maximum possible) yet the impact on overall success probability would be at most 1%. Resources increasing the success probabilities of the riskier paths produce higher returns.

Maximizing Probability of Success

A variety of actions that can be taken to increase the probability of success of high-risk critical paths. Some are described below:

1. Work on riskiest critical paths first

Attack the riskiest critical paths early in the execution phase. This provides more time for pursuing alternate solutions if an approach runs into trouble. Note this is opposite the strategy people often use to take school exams. There, one solves the easiest problems first to lock in as many correct scores as possible, and then spend the remaining time attempting the harder problems. The difference in business is a project is successful or not - partial credits are not important if overall objectives are not achieved.

2. Supplement weak critical paths with parallel paths

The probability of success in critical paths can be enhanced with parallel solution approaches. For design projects, this might take the form of parallel design teams. Each solution approach has its own probability of success. *Failure* of the critical path would only happen if *all* parallel solution approaches were to fail. Since the likelihood of that happening is lower than if only one solution approach were used, the probability of success is higher. For example, if step B in in Fig. 3.5 (a) is a high-risk critical path step, the risk of that step can be lowered by adding the parallel solution B1 shown in Fig. 3.5 (b).

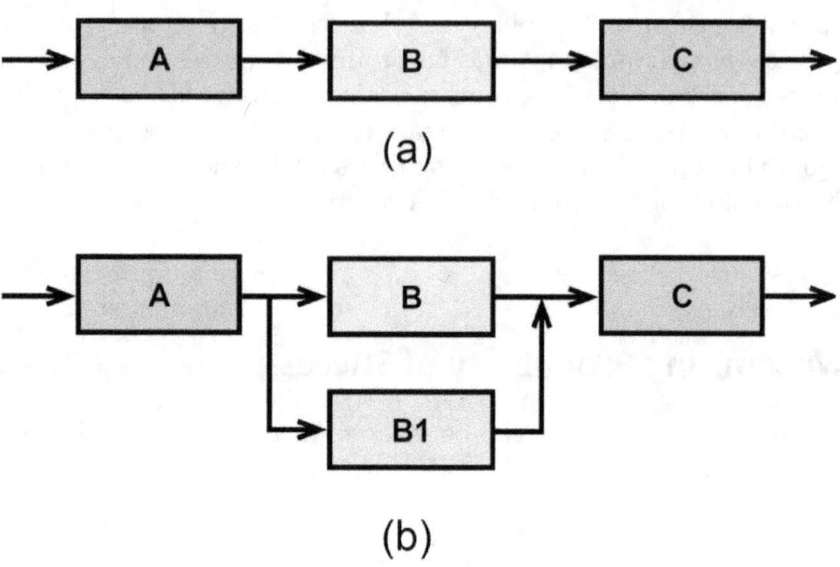

(a)

(b)

Figure 3.5 Adding parallel approaches to the riskiest paths to reduce risk.

If the parallel approaches are independent (i.e., depend on entirely different factors), the combined probability of success is easily estimated by subtracting the probability of *both* B and B1 failing from one. For example, if the probabilities of success of B and B1 are 0.6 (60%) and 0.4 (40%), respectively. The probability of both failing is (1-0.6) X (1-0.4) = .24 or 24%. Since this is necessary for the parallel combination to fail, the probability of success of the parallel combination is (1-.24) = .76 or 76%, well above the 60% and 40% of B or B1 alone.

3. Avoid high-risk critical paths

This involves examining the project plan to find alternate solution strategies to avoid the riskiest critical paths. This could include strategies where lower risk critical paths are traded for somewhat higher risk critical paths to avoid the highest risk critical paths. Such tradeoffs capitalize on the fact that changing risk in low-risk paths has a lesser effect on project success than changing risk in high-risk paths.

For example, suppose in one strategy we have the critical paths shown in Fig. 3.6 (a), where the probability of success of each of the critical paths is denoted by the numbers shown above each box. Clearly A and C are low-risk and B is high-risk. Fig. 3.6 (b) shows an alternate strategy, one where B is replaced by two lower risk paths B1 and C1, and A and C are replaced with higher risk paths A1 and D1. Notice the combination in (b) has lower overall risk.

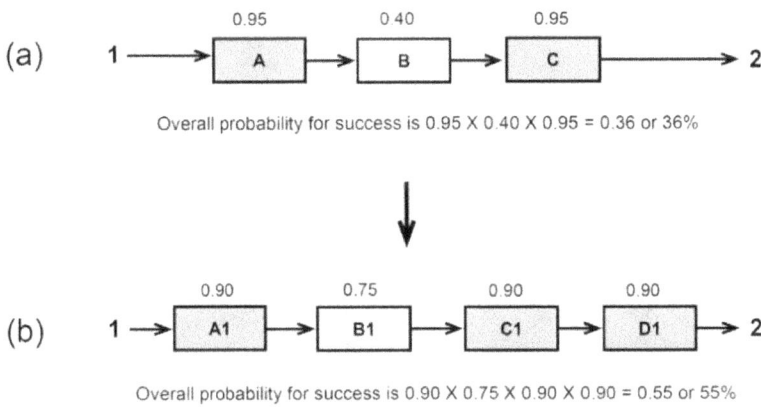

Figure 3.6   Alternate strategies with a different mix of risks may be better.

These concepts also apply to projects with long-term goals. Recall earlier in this chapter we pointed out project uncertainty increases the further into the future our target objectives. Pursuing such goals through a series of incremental short-term projects can often lower risk since uncertainty is less in short-term projects. However, to meet long term goals *all* interim goals would have to be successful. So, this would be a better approach only if the combined success probabilities of the shorter-term projects is lower than the success probability of the single long-term project.

Summary

One cannot predict the precise consequences of any management decision. The best any manager can do is choose plans that maximize the likelihood of achieving objectives. These are plans with the least amount of uncertainty (lowest risk).

Decreasing risk in high-risk critical paths decreases overall project risk more than decreasing risk in low-risk critical paths. Consequently, reducing risk in the highest risk critical paths is one of the better ways of reducing project uncertainty.

4. Conservation of Time/Resources

Two factors limit action choices in every project: *time* and *resources*. Every project has a deadline - a date after which completion of goals no longer achieves business objectives. For example, a project aimed at enhancing engineering tools for designing the next computer chip will be far less useful if the improved tools are delivered after the engineers have completed their design. The existence of a deadline means there is a time limit for completing every project.

Likewise, there are also limits to resources for every project. Staffing and money are always limited. Intellectual property, equipment, and manufacturing capacity may also be limiters. Collectively, these limiters restrict the solution space. This is depicted in Fig. 4.1, where resource limits are collectively represented on a single horizontal axis (a more detailed representation would have many such axes, one for each resource limit) and the time represented on the vertical axis. Only project strategies inside the shaded region will meet the time and resource limitations of the project.

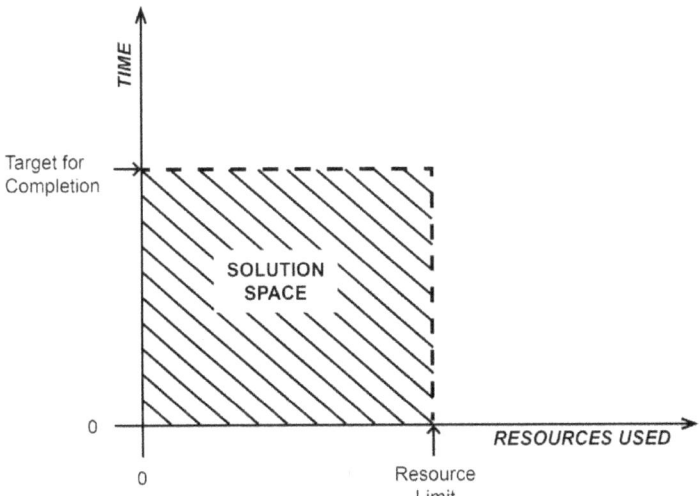

Figure 4.1 Project solutions are restricted by time and resources.

Since every activity takes time and time is limited, every activity means less time for other activities. Managers need to trade-off activities when making plans to ensure the actions they choose are ones that contribute most to project success. All actions are not equal (see Fig 4.2). Recall from Chapter 3 where we pointed out actions affecting high-risk critical paths contribute more to success than actions affecting low-risk critical paths.

"Have you thought of how you are going to connect up to Highway 97?"
"Not yet, we've been too busy making this section of road the best ever"

Figure 4.2 All activities are not equal in value.

And what if the project plan predicts goal targets will not be met? This would be an irrational plan since failure is the target. While one can hope a project will proceed better than planned – that is gambling on an unlikely outcome. One should only consider plans that result in success if everything goes as planned.

Trading Time and Resources

Time and resources are interrelated limiters. For example, if resources were unlimited, we could apply infinite resources to a task to compensate for time limitations (see Fig. 4.3). Likewise, infinite time can compensate for insufficient resources. Of course, in the real world neither is unlimited.

"We were falling behind schedule. Then they called in the Army..."

Figure 4.3   Resources and time are interrelated – more resources can speed projects.

Changing time or resources is usually an upper management decision since such changes affect resources available for other projects. For example, increasing money for one project may leave too little for other projects. Upper management's job is ensuring plans maximize the success of the larger organization.

For a given execution strategy, the minimum time a worker can complete a job is the sum of the execution times for each of the subtasks that worker must complete to perform that job. This is the *minimum,* since the worker will also be spending time on other activities, such as waiting for parts, communicating with coworkers, taking rest breaks, etc. Consequently, the sum of the execution times for all job subtasks cannot be greater than the time available for the job.

In many cases this time limit will determine what resources can be used. If time limits are short, resources more suited to longer-range approaches should be avoided. Resources need to be tailored to immediate project needs (see Fig. 4.4).

"Help. It's coming apart! Quick, hand me the screwdriver!"

"No, a box wrench is better for those screws. Let's see, it's here somewhere..."

Figure 4.4   Resources need to be tailored to time schedules.

The Cost of Multi-Tasking

Having people work on more than one job at a time should be avoided whenever possible, since alternating between different jobs adds overhead (e.g., time to reorient mindset, time to record and retrieve data, time to switch tools and materials, ...), leaving less time for core tasks.

This is illustrated in Fig. 4.5 below. In Approach-(a) resources are switched back and forth between Job-A (boxes A1, A2, ...) and Job-B (boxes B1, B2, ...), whereas in Approach-(b) Job-A is completed before Job-B is started. The thin vertical bars depict the overhead of switching between Job-A and Job-B. Since there is more switching in the multiplexed Approach-(a) versus the sequential Approach-(b), all else being equal, the multiplexed approach will always take more time. Notice not only does the sequential Approach-(b) take less total time, but *both* Job-A and Job-B complete earlier in Approach-(b).

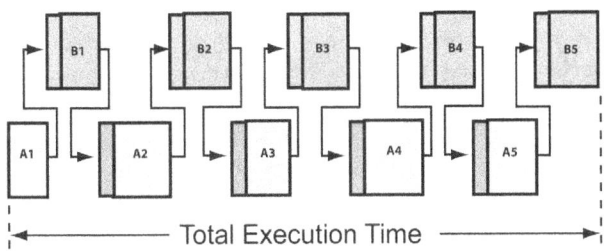

a) MULTIPLEXED JOB EXECUTION APPROACH

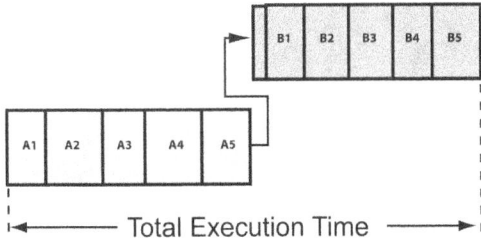

b) SEQUENTIAL JOB EXECUTION APPROACH

Figure 4.5 Why multi-tasking takes more time.

All else being equal, it is more efficient to have people complete one job before starting another job.

This assumes that the worker can spend all his or her time working productively on a single job. If there are significant periods when that is not possible (e.g., from delays in getting parts or approvals) then obviously it would be better to have the worker pursue other tasks while waiting.

Note that the advantage of single-tasking versus multi-tasking is only true for *independent* subtasks, whose execution are not dependent on each other. If the subtasks are interdependent, the multiplexed approach might be preferable since it allows for faster adjustment of interdependent subtasks if problems are encountered. In practice, interdependent tasks are probably better viewed as parts of a larger single task.

Methods for Speeding Execution

Speeding execution is always desirable. Faster execution frees up more time for unanticipated problems and increases the likelihood of goal deadlines being met. Faster execution can also reduce costs by freeing up resources for other projects. Some techniques for speeding execution are listed below:

1. Parallel Execution

Execution can be speeded up by spreading subtasks across multiple teams to *execute tasks in parallel*. This works best when the parallel tasks are independent of each other. This is equivalent to adding additional resources to shorten execution time.

2. Solution Re-Use

Adapting past solutions instead of developing entirely new ones can reduce tasks in a project and speed execution. Such techniques are widely practiced in software development. Developing reusable solutions does add overhead, however (e.g., from additional documentation, adoption of standardized interfaces, etc.).

3. Focusing Objectives

Focusing project objectives to only those absolutely needed for project success can speed execution. While it is tempting to incorporate multiple objectives in a single project, doing so increases the number of tasks needed to be successful. For example, introducing the next-generation chip manufacturing process at the same time a next-generation chip design is introduced increases the number of high-risk tasks that must succeed for product success, increasing chances for failure. The probability of success would be higher if the new manufacturing process was first proven on an existing (low risk) chip design, and then on new chip designs after the manufacturing process has been debugged and stabilized.

Advantages of Starting Early

Starting a project early increases chances for project success since it provides more time for project execution. This is equivalent to increasing the solution window for a project. Stretching out the available time means more time for learning and more time for course corrections if difficulties are encountered. Conversely, the closer we are to project delivery time, the fewer the options in event of problems. The underlying concept can be summarized as:

For a given objective, the probability of project success decreases the closer the project delivery date is to the start date.

This is the rationale for long-range research and development programs. More time for projects means lower risk. However, this also means committing resources over a longer period and increased costs - reducing resources for shorter-term projects. Nevertheless, long-range projects are usually the only way to make major leaps in progress.

Insufficient investment in long-range programs can result in an environment where project plans are continually disrupted by unexpected problems. This can lead to reactive "fire-fighting" modes of operation, where unexpected crises consume all resources, further starving long-term programs. This is a vicious cycle, one that is difficult to escape from once begun, and one that can cause an organization to quickly become uncompetitive. Fig. 4.6 depicts a homeowner trapped in a "fire-fighting mode". Management judgment is critical for maintaining the balance between short and long-range programs.

"I know I should strengthen my seawall, but I've been too busy holding my house together."

Figure 4.6 Focusing on only short-range problems can be hazardous.

Resource Cliffs

In this last section we will discuss resource limitations in high growth environments. Specifically, we will discuss the problems of growth when it is dependent on the growing consumption of limited resources.

One example of this is the growing consumption of oil as world populations and economies grow. Since the amount of oil is limited (formed from millions of years of decaying plants and animals), this is a situation that is unsustainable over the long term since the world will eventually run out of affordable oil. Growing concerns about global warming and the emission of carbon dioxide also limit the utilization of such fossil fuels.

Resource cliffs could also limit the growth of electric vehicles. The limited availability of lithium, cobalt, neodymium and other materials used in the construction of batteries and electric motors may limit the growth of such vehicles unless manufacturers find alternate sources or technologies.

In business, money is often the universal measure of resource; since in principle one can purchase whatever resources one needs if one has enough money. While this may be true, if real resources become scarce they will become prohibitively expensive to use. Thus, businesses need to keep track of the availability of actual resources not just money, especially if their growth is dependent on growing consumption of those resources.

The basic problem is illustrated in Fig. 4.7.

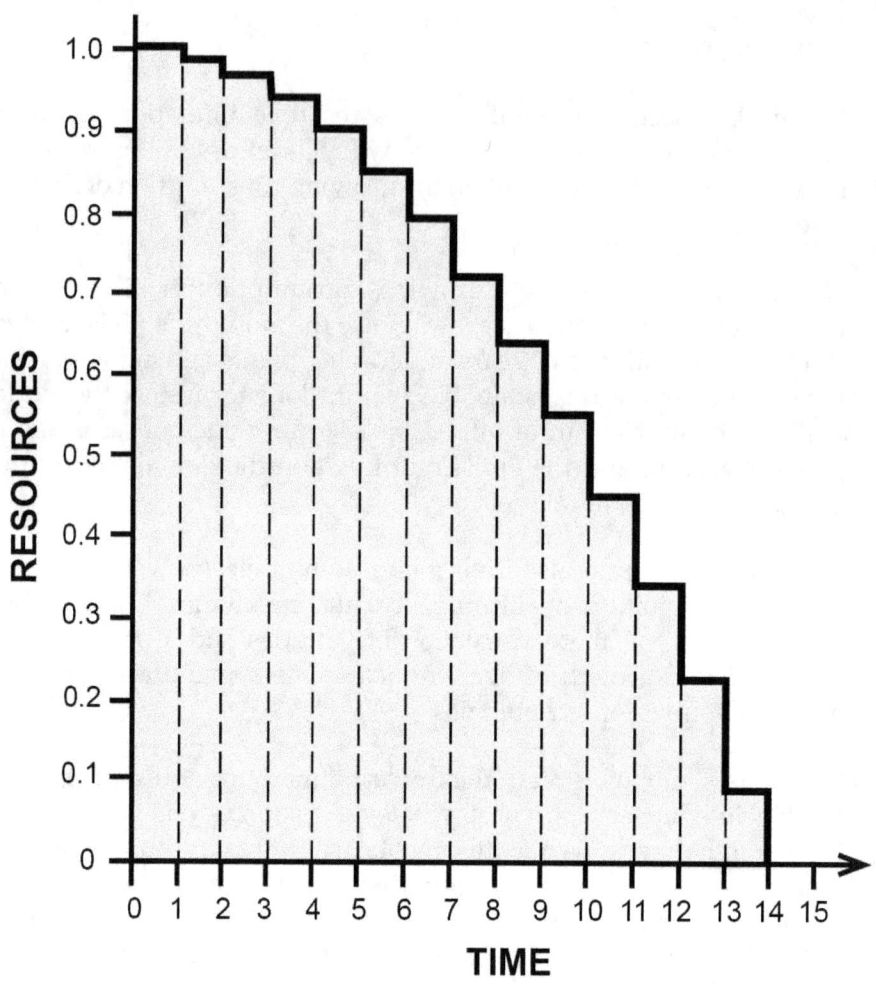

Figure 4.7 Example resource cliff.

This example depicts a growing business whose consumption of a limited resource is proportional to the business's growth. In this example, the business consumes 1% of a resource during the first month and doubles its business in the first month to consume 2% of the original resources. Next month it grows by the same month-to-month increment and consumes 3% of the original resources, and so on for each succeeding month. Since the growth of resource usage per month is only 1% of the initial resource, one might think the resource should last many years. However, since the business is consuming ever-larger amounts per month, the remaining resource is depleted at an ever-growing pace and is in fact totally depleted by the 14th month. This is what I call a *"resource cliff"* – the time when resources are effectively used up.

Resource cliffs also apply to money. For example, if initial growth is from selling products at a loss, product plans need to show break-even (the time when income exceeds expenses) before all the money is depleted, otherwise the business will fail.

In general, if there is limited availability of necessary components or raw materials, one needs to analyze whether the business will be sufficiently profitable before resource cliffs are reached. Starting and growing a new business entails significant costs and time. It is important that businesses recoup those costs and generate a reasonable return from investments of time and money before resource cliffs are reached. If resource limitations affect a whole industry (not just one company) resource cliffs will be reached even earlier.

Resource cliffs affect how large businesses dependent on such resources can grow. These limitations need to be incorporated in strategic business plans to ensure transitions to different products or services are made before resource cliffs are reached. The key message is that careful planning is essential when resource cliffs are limiters.

"Hand me more food, it's working! Their
attention is on the food and not us..."

Figure 4.8 Maybe a different plan would have been better.

Summary

Time and resources are limited in all projects. Since every activity takes time and resources, managers need to carefully select project activities that contribute most to project success.

Worker multi-tasking is usually less efficient than working on single tasks sequentially. Projects can be speeded up using parallel project teams and by reusing previous solutions. Except for simple projects, the probability of project success decreases the closer the target completion date is to the start date. Projects started well in advance of needs (long-range projects) are often necessary to tackle difficult projects. Planners need to be aware of resource cliffs that can limit longer-term growth plans.

The limitations of time and resources is illustrated in the hypothetical situation in Fig. 4.9 below. The driver needs to get to a ferry before it leaves. The driver discovers his fuel is low and knows there are no gas stations before the ferry terminal. If he drives slowly, he could conserve enough fuel to make it to the ferry terminal, but if he drives too slowly he will miss the ferry. He also knows he could get to the ferry on time if he drove at the maximum speed - but doing so will cause him to certainly run out of gas before reaching the ferry.

Figure 4.9 Problem: how to get to the ferry on time with low fuel?

So, what is the driver to do? If there is a solution, it will be driving fast enough to get to the ferry just before it leaves, as this meets the time constraint (one limiter) and pushes the other limiter (fuel) the least. Provided the driver has a map showing the distance, this speed can be estimated. The driver would, however, be wise to allow some additional time for unforeseen traffic problems and update his calculation of the needed speed after encountering such problems. Notice this strategy does not guarantee success (i.e., making it to the ferry before it leaves) but maximizes the probability of doing so, which is the best that can be done.

5. Information Turns

Information is "gold" for managers. Since all decisions are based on available information, all else being equal, the manager with the most information can make better decisions than his or her competitors.

Figure 5.1   Information is manager's "gold" for making decisions.

Information can be divided into two classes: *public domain* and *proprietary*.

Public domain information is information that has been disclosed openly in books, publications, talks, and products. It is information that is available to all competitors. It includes information that is imparted in schools and universities. Managers need to make maximal use of public domain information since their competitors have access to that same information.

Proprietary information, on the other hand, is information that is available only to selected organizations or companies. Building a repository of proprietary information can be key for establishing a competitive edge. Companies can generate such information themselves or purchase it from others.

Mining Existing Information

The challenge is the mountain of available information is enormous. How does one find the most relevant information, given only a small fraction will be useful for any given project?

Figure 5.2 No single individual can see or understand all the information.

This is the information mining and filtering process, a process that relies heavily on human judgment. One needs to know where to look and what to ignore, and how to analyze the information that is found. People select information based on their own orientation, biases, experiences, and training. Various people may interpret and filter the same information very differently. One manager might ignore information that another manager finds important, yet both may have good reasons based on their own perspectives. Combining different viewpoints broadens the overview of available information.

Figure 5.3. More viewpoints can be useful.

Just as project goals have time and resource limits (Chapter 4), there are limits to the amount of new information a single person can absorb. The easiest way to process more information is to enlist the help of others – especially those with different experiences and perspectives. Hiring experts (employees or contractors) in areas outside the manager's expertise is especially useful. Talking to prospective customers to learn what they view is important is also valuable. In general, enlisting others in the information filtering process is one of the best ways of reducing the likelihood important information is missed.

Generating New Information

So far, we have been talking about selecting relevant information from available information - but what about generating new information?

New information is typically generated through a basic three-step process:

1. Experiments performed
2. Results analyzed
3. Information extracted

I will refer to such processes as *"Information Turns"*. This is depicted in the flow diagram shown in Fig. 5.4, which shows new information being generated with each experimental cycle. The circular path shows new information being used to define subsequent experiments. This is a variant of the old saying "you learn by doing". Examples of experimental cycles include tests of prototype products, exhibitions of novel works of art, and product trials in new markets.

As we learn more, uncertainty decreases and predictability improves. Furthermore, new learning provides us information about unexplored areas – expanding our solution options.

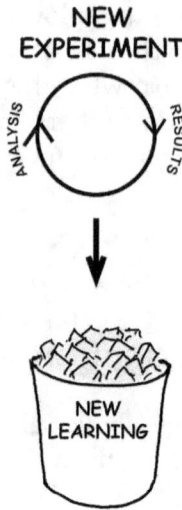

Figure 5.4. Information Turn flow diagram

Fig. 5.5 below contrasts the two ways of obtaining information.

Figure 5.5 Two ways of obtaining information: mining existing information and creating new information.

Value of More Information Turns

The *number* of information turns in a project is an important parameter. All else being equal, more information turns mean more learning and more new information. More information means reduced uncertainty (less risk from unexpected problems) and expanded solution space (discovery of more solution paths for achieving objectives).

Generally speaking:

Learning increases with the number of information turns

This means the probability of achieving objectives will often be greater when plans are executed in many incremental steps versus one large step, since the information turns in each step provide learning that can be used to optimize subsequent steps.

Value of Faster Information Turns

The time for executing an information turn is an important parameter - since shorter times allow for more information turns. The time for executing information turns determines the learning time scale.

Learning time scales depend on the type of experiment. For example, pharmaceutical trials involve long experiments, since the effectiveness of new drugs often requires long-term testing on animal and human subjects. In contrast, software experiments can be carried out very quickly, as changes to computer code can be tested almost instantly. This is why software developments occur at a much faster rate than medical developments. In general:

Shorter information turns facilitate faster learning

This has been particularly evident in the digital electronics revolution, where new electronic product developments are increasingly driven by software than hardware. This has accelerated the introduction of new and improved electronic products. Engineers routinely use computer-aided design (CAD) tools to explore and test new designs in minutes what would have taken months of testing using laboratory experiments. Word processing programs allow writers to instantly test, revise, and polish writing on computer screens. Digital cameras allow photographers to see their results immediately and experiment with alternate compositions without costly photographic film. When objectives can be quantified, computers can even be programmed to find optimum solutions automatically.

Another consequence has been the development of even more powerful computers. This, in turn, has enabled ever-increasing acceleration of software information turns.

Fig. 5.6 shows why many short information turns are often better than one long information turn that tries to resolve all questions in a single experiment. An approach using multiple short information turns not only generates more information but generates it earlier. This allows unanticipated problems to be found earlier, increasing chances for success.

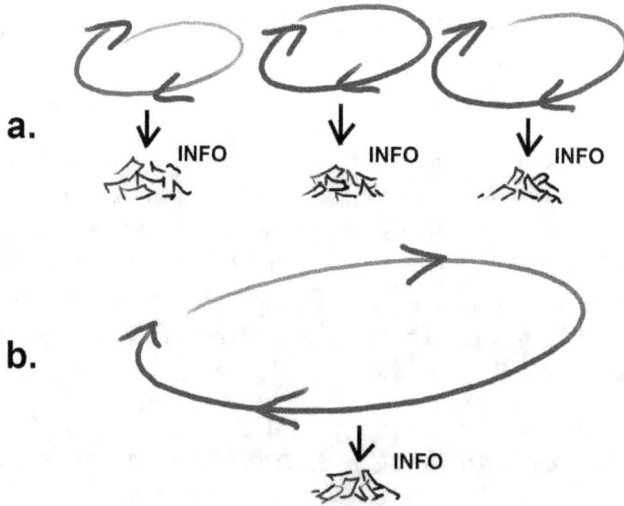

Figure 5.6   (a) Multiple info turns versus (b) a single info turn.

A real-world example is the launching of a business venture to introduce a family of new products. One could commit all resources (money) to the manufacture, marketing, and distribution of the family of products in a single launch. This is equivalent to counting on a single information turn to provide all the learning needed for success. However, if the products have problems or fail to get the desired customer reception, the business will be left with huge inventories of unsold products. They may also be left with insufficient money to correct strategies, increasing the likelihood the business will fail.

A better approach would be to enter new markets gradually with a limited set of products (the most promising ones) to test business assumptions. This is equivalent to proceeding using several shorter information turns. This allows a business to build learning gradually and address unexpected problems while money is readily available.

Business Planning for More Information Turns

Shortening information turns is also why formal business planning is recommended for new business ventures. In its most basic form, business plans are made up of the following components:

1. Definition of product and services to be offered

2. Identification of current and future competitors.

3. Assessment of the competitive advantages of proposed offerings.

4. Identification of target customers that would be attracted to those offerings.

5. Marketing strategy for reaching target customers

6. Cash-flow analysis using above assumptions to project when break-even and profitability targets will be reached.

This process is depicted in the following flow diagram:

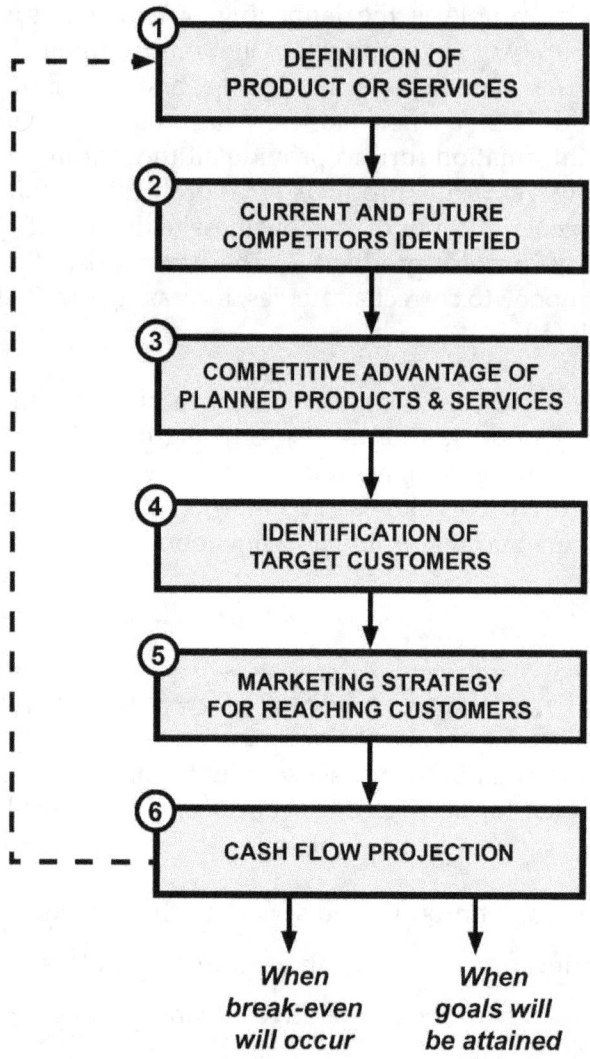

Figure 5.7 Basic elements of a business plan

Business plans allow entrepreneurs to try out different business scenarios before committing significant resources. Specifically, they allow them to "test" different business plans on paper (as many as several a day) to determine which plans are most promising. Each of these analyses is essentially an experiment, albeit a theoretical one, that generates learning. Such analyses can help identify the best plan given available information. In contrast, an entrepreneur that simply "jumps in" without planning is gambling that his or her initial plan is the one that will succeed. Given there are many ways of accomplishing an objective, the probability that the entrepreneur will have chosen the best approach is small. If competitors have selected a better approach, the new business starts at a major disadvantage. This is the reason why business planning is strongly encouraged for people starting new businesses.

Designing Information Turns

Of course, learning from information turns depends on the *design* of the experiments. Experiments need to be designed to generate the maximum amount of new information for an expenditure of resources. For example, testing a new consumer product by showing it to engineering associates will probably not provide much new information. A better experiment would be to test market the product with a random group of target customers. The best experiments push the boundaries of learning by exploring areas where one has little information. This can be summarized as:

The more unexplored areas tested, the more useful the information turns.

Again, some managers find it uncomfortable poking into unfamiliar areas and confine experiments to areas where they have expertise. Doing so, however, provides less learning.

Figure 5.8 By limiting his exploration to nearby hills, Explorer-1 (in the foreground) is unable to find a shorter way to get from A to B. In contrast, the Explorer-2 explores beyond those hills and finds a shorter route from A to B.

Careful *analysis of experimental results* is also needed to extract maximum learning from an information turn. The analysis plan needs to be part of the design of the information turn to ensure experiments will generate the needed information.

Information turns are most useful when they have *clear objectives* (e.g., test a specific solution, calibrate models, etc.) and are not overly general. Such information turns are more likely to produce the needed information quickly and with fewer resources.

Information for Supervision

Of course, managers also need information to carry out supervisory responsibilities – not just for project planning. Employees are concerned about many things beyond an organization's strategic goals. They include understanding their assignments, job satisfaction, professional growth, interactions with employees, etc. While these are not explicit elements in project plans, they can affect project execution and success or failure of plans. Addressing employee concerns enhances morale and minimizes employee turnover.

Managers are not mind readers, even though employees often believe managers "ought to know" their concerns without being explicitly told. It is essential that managers establish working rapport with their employees so issues can be discussed openly. Regularly scheduled 1-on-1 meetings between managers and their employees are one of the best ways of establishing such rapport. Managers can facilitate this by formally scheduling regular 1-on-1 meetings with each of their direct reports, with time reserved for listening to their personal issues.

Visionaries Also Need Information

In this chapter, we have been stressing the value of information and how it can be used to analyze needs and solve problems. But what about visionaries, people who can foresee the future and predict market trends before other people? Is information as important for them?

Visionaries still make use of available information. Their ability to extract more from the same information amplifies the value of knowledge. The importance of maximizing information for making decisions applies equally to them.

Summary

Information is fuel for managers. All else being equal, the manager with the most information is better positioned for finding the best solutions.

Information can be either public domain or proprietary. Effective use of public domain information requires the assistance of additional people, ones with expertise and experience in different areas. Proprietary information, or information available only to selective companies or organizations, can be used to build competitive advantages.

New information is generated through a basic three-step experimental process called an information turn. Project plans that provide for more information turns are desirable, as the incremental information provided from each information turn aids execution and plan refinement. Information turns need to be designed carefully to maximize useful information.

Effective supervision of employees requires being aware of employee personal concerns. Active solicitation of such concerns by supervisors in scheduled 1-on-1 meetings is a useful tactic for obtaining such information. Such meetings are another form of information turn.

The flow diagram in Fig. 5.9 depicts the flow and generation of new information in information turns.

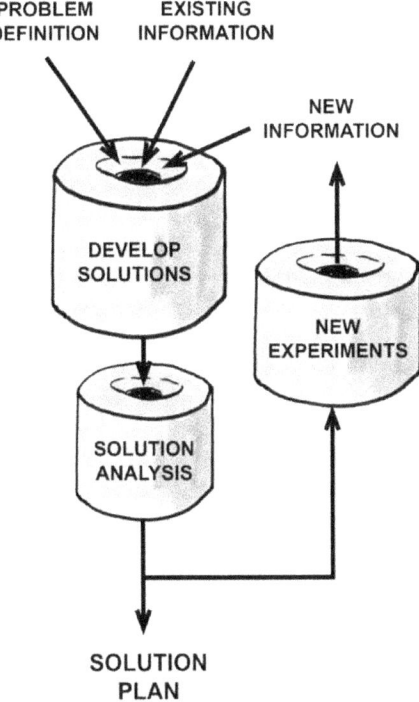

Figure 5.9 Information turns generate new information. More information reduces uncertainty, improving the likelihood of plan success.

6. Learning Curves

Imagine you are an explorer who has just found an opening to a hidden cave. You break through the opening and shine your light inside and smile on seeing gold nuggets everywhere. You quickly collect visible nuggets, carrying them out in your backpack. You then re-enter the cave and examine it more carefully and locate gold nuggets hidden in nooks and crannies. Afterwards you start examining the walls of the cave more closely, scraping surfaces to locate hidden gold veins. You leave the cave and return the following day with a pickaxe and shovel and start excavating the rock around the gold veins. The gold veins broaden then shrink with the excavation, and after several weeks of excavating they dwindle and disappear. With money from the gold, you hire a professional crew with hydraulic drilling equipment and sensitive gold detection instruments to dig deeper into the mountain following the dwindling veins to their very end. After the veins disappear you have the mountain refuse trucked to a crushing plant to retrieve gold fragments that were missed. Each ensuing action is more expensive and produces progressively less gold. Eventually they fail to produce enough gold to offset increasing costs and the gold mine is abandoned.

The cartoon below (Fig. 6.1) depicts the successive stages of learning in the cave. Successive exploration trips require increasing effort and yield less and less new learning (new gold).

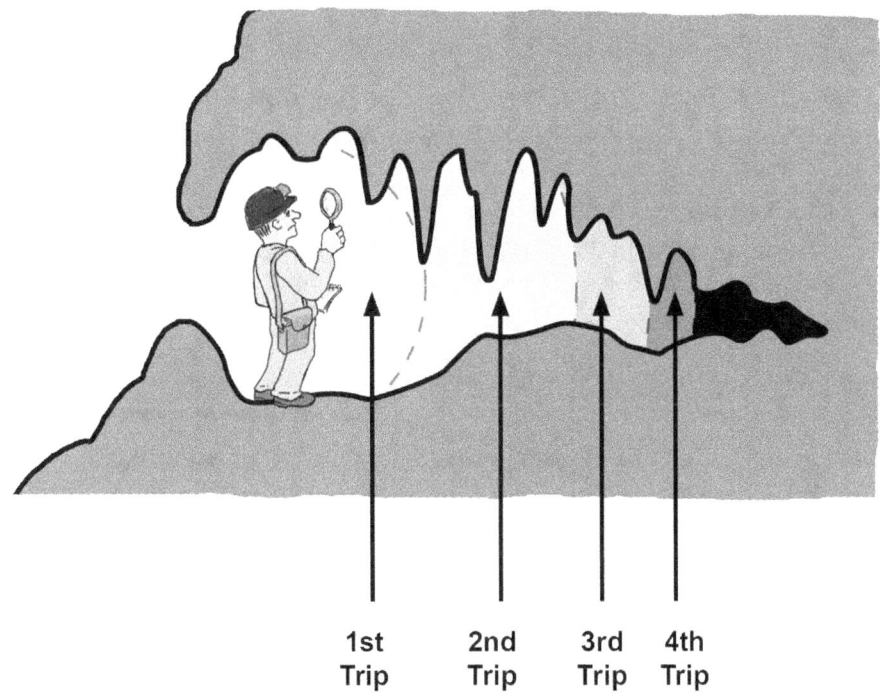

1st   2nd   3rd   4th
Trip   Trip   Trip   Trip

Figure 6.1 Successive explorations require more effort and yield smaller returns. The concentric shaded regions depict the amount of new gold gained from successive explorations.

This story illustrates a general observation:

Learning is greatest at the start of a new endeavor and declines over time.

In the case of the cave explorer, gold was most easily found when the person first entered the cave. Initially the exploration yielded quick returns (i.e., lots of gold). After the surface nuggets were collected, further exploration took more time as the remaining gold was hidden in crevices and less accessible regions of the cave. As more gold was removed, the remaining gold were in areas increasingly difficult to access – namely deeper in the mountain. These required more expensive mining techniques and yielded less and less gold. Eventually, the cost of finding additional gold exceeded the returns.

The underlying concept is:

What is left to learn in an area declines as we accumulate learning in that area.

This trend is represented by the basic *Learning Curve* shown below in Fig. 6.2, where the vertical *"LEARNING"* axis measures the *accumulated* learning over time.

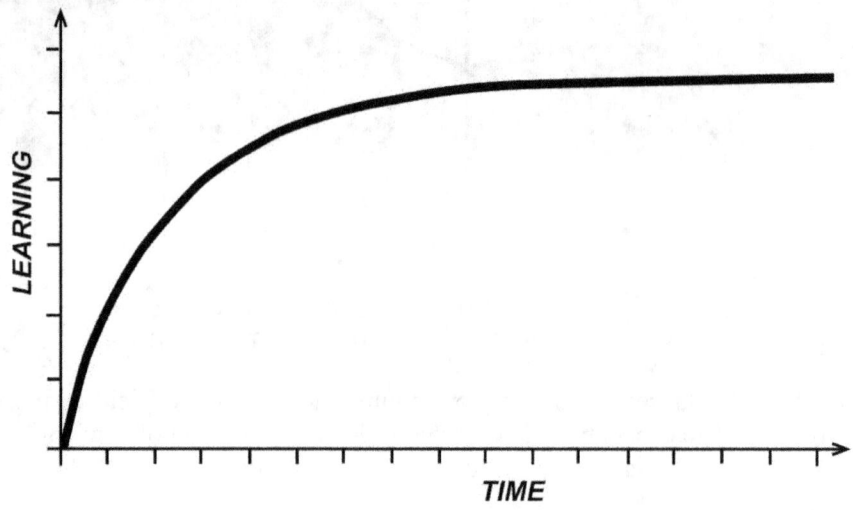

Figure 6.2   Basic learning curve showing the growth of learning is greatest at the beginning.

The exponential shape of this curve stems from a simple assumption: *the rate of new learning is proportional to what is left to learn.* The flattening of the learning curve over time reflects the fact that it takes longer and longer to discover new information as the amount of undiscovered information shrinks.   Eventually it will take an impracticable amount of time to learn any new information. When this occurs, we say the learning curve has saturated – meaning there is little left to learn.

An analogous example in business is a company selling a new

product. Initially, sales grow rapidly, as many people discover and purchase the product. After some time, sales slow as most people who would buy the product have already done so. The company lowers the price of the product and sales pick up again, where increased sales compensate for the lower profit per unit. After some time, people who would buy at the lower price have done so and sales again drop off. The company hesitates to lower the price even more, as profits are already marginal, and the additional customers might not offset costs. In this example, the "learning" is the discovery of customers. As more and more customers are found, the number left to find declines – a classical learning curve behavior. Notice, like the gold mine example, the initial customers were not only easy to find, but were willing to pay premium prices. Later customers required more work – just as in our gold mine example.

Note that learning curves represent the time-averaged rate of accumulated learning. At any given time, actual learning may be above or below the representative learning curve since there will be instances when learning may be especially fast or slow. In the previous gold mine example, an "above" situation would be the discovery of a cave pocket where nuggets were especially numerous. Fig. 6.3 shows how actual learning might appear superimposed on the time-averaged learning curve.

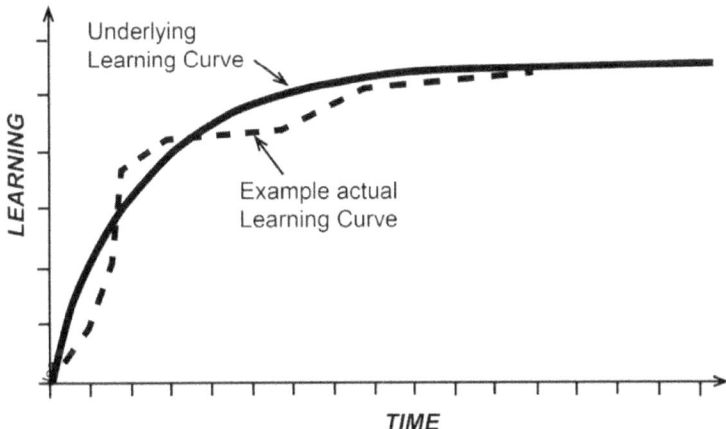

Figure 6.3 Actual rates of learning will vary around the basic learning curve, which represents the average rate of accumulated learning over time.

The concept of learning curves has profound implications in business.

Profitability and Learning Curves

The profit potential of any endeavor depends on its entry point on the learning curve. Products or services in early stages of learning have lots of room for improvement. This means significantly improved versions of products or services can be easily developed and sold to people who have purchased earlier versions. Since the customer base would also be growing (as more people learn of the offerings), this can be a period of rapid profit growth. In contrast, products and services that are near the mature end of their learning curves can be improved only little, so existing customers are less likely to purchase new versions. The market will eventually shrink to mostly customers replacing worn-out units or consumed products (e.g., food). This translates to declining profitability at the mature end of learning curves. These trends are depicted in Figure 6.4 below:

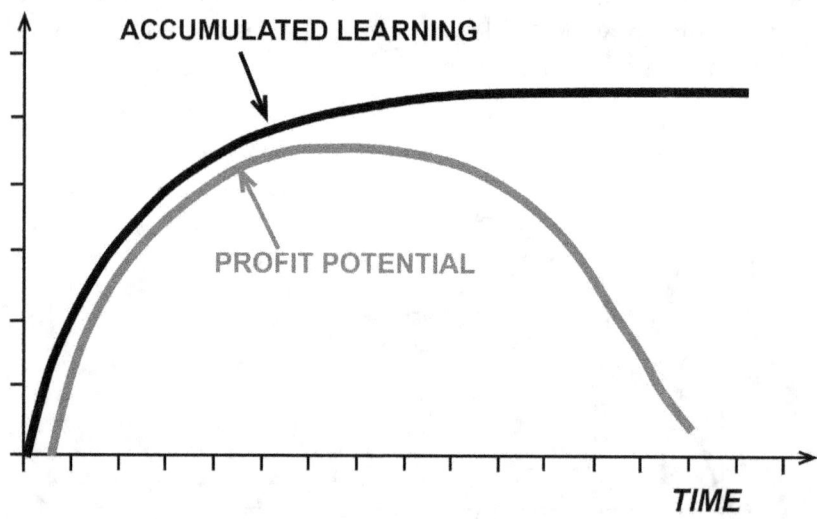

Figure 6.4 Comparison of a learning curve and its associated profit potential.

This figure also shows the profit potential of any idea is typically low at the beginning, since it takes time and money to develop a new idea (i.e., build learning) before saleable products or services can be made available. Profits will be greatest when there is strong demand for the products and the customer base is large. Both will shrink as the product matures (improvements become smaller) and competition grows (customer base becomes diluted).

Business Strategies Have Finite Lifetimes

All business strategies are governed by learning curves. For a given endeavor (i.e., a given business), the benefits from pursuing a particular business strategy declines over time. Eventually the benefits will be too small to warrant further pursuit of the approach and we say the learning curve has **saturated** or flattened out. I will refer to the time from the start of the learning curve to when it reaches 90% of its maximum as the "**lifetime**" of the learning curve (see Fig. 6.5).

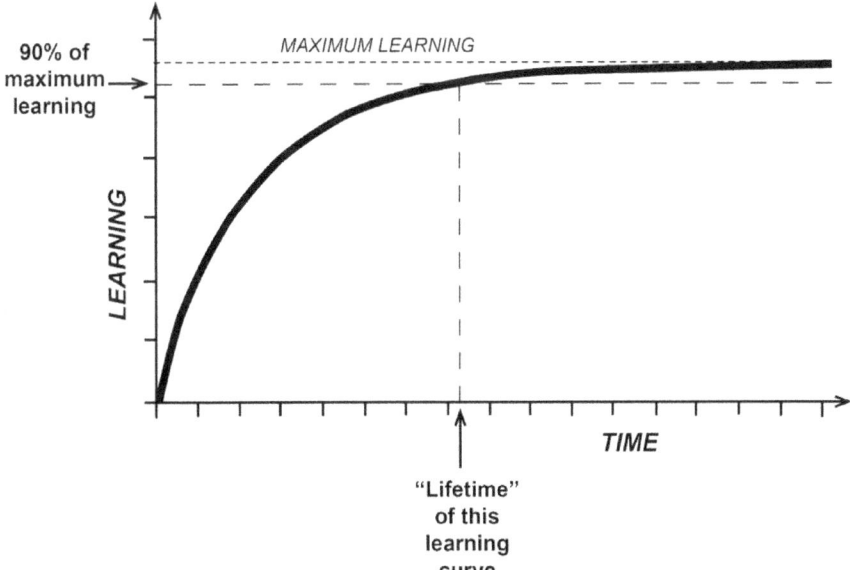

Figure 6.5 The useful "lifetime" of a learning curve is reached when approximately 90% of the available learning has been extracted.

This is a common situation in product design. All designs can be improved with additional engineering (made better, cheaper, etc.). Initial efforts utilize approaches that produce big improvements using few resources (i.e., the "easier" improvements). Since the easiest improvements are made first, subsequent improvements are increasingly difficult, with diminishing returns. At some point the cost of making further improvements exceeds business gains and further development no longer makes sense.

Dependence on Learning Curve Entry Point

In most business situations, we enter endeavors that other companies are already pursuing, namely we build on existing learning. In such situations, our participation begins some distance down an existing learning curve, not at the beginning. Where we enter a learning curve is important. The further down a learning curve our entry point, the lower potential new learning (returns), and the sooner we reach saturation. The time between when we enter a learning curve and the time to when it saturates is referred to as the **remaining lifetime** in Fig. 6.6 below.

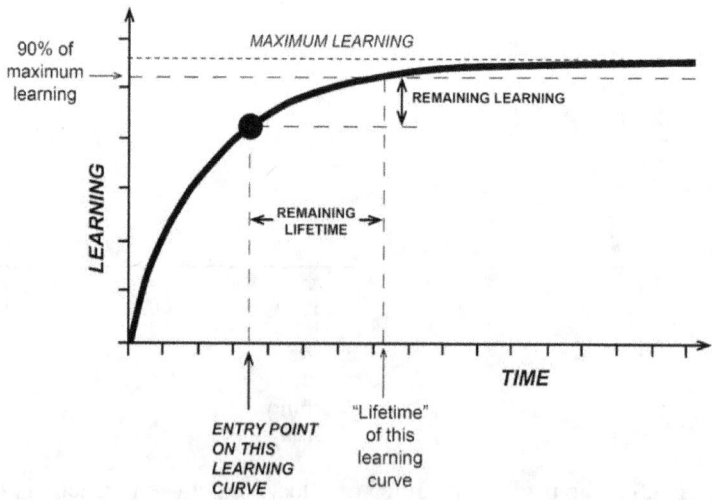

Figure 6.6 For a given endeavor, the *remaining lifetime* and *remaining new learning* depends on one's entry point on the learning curve.

Notice that the earlier we enter a learning curve the greater the amount of potential new learning and potential returns. However, the risks are also greater, as there is less data, and it is harder to predict the eventual shape of the learning curve.

Nevertheless, entering a learning curve near its end of life is probably least rewarding. Although such learning curves are established and supported by extensive data, they are also the ones with the lowest growth prospects. They are also directions probably pursued by multiple competitors, whose collective learning accelerates saturation of the learning curve.

Continued Success Requires New Learning Curves

Learning curves are relevant to all development activities – from detailed product improvement to long-range strategic planning. Companies who are pioneers in the use of new technologies are early entrants on new learning curves. Their early entry enables them to reap benefits and develop expertise before competitors.

That advantage can also become a trap, however. It can lead pioneering companies to pursue the same approaches long after learning curves have started saturating, causing them to devote excessive resources for diminishing returns. This may allow competitor companies pursuing alternate approaches (new learning curves) to leapfrog a company's product lines. This often happens when competitors pursue emerging technologies with more future growth. New technologies that obsolete existing approaches (existing learning curves) are often referred to as "disruptive technologies".

Fig. 6.7 illustrates this hazard.

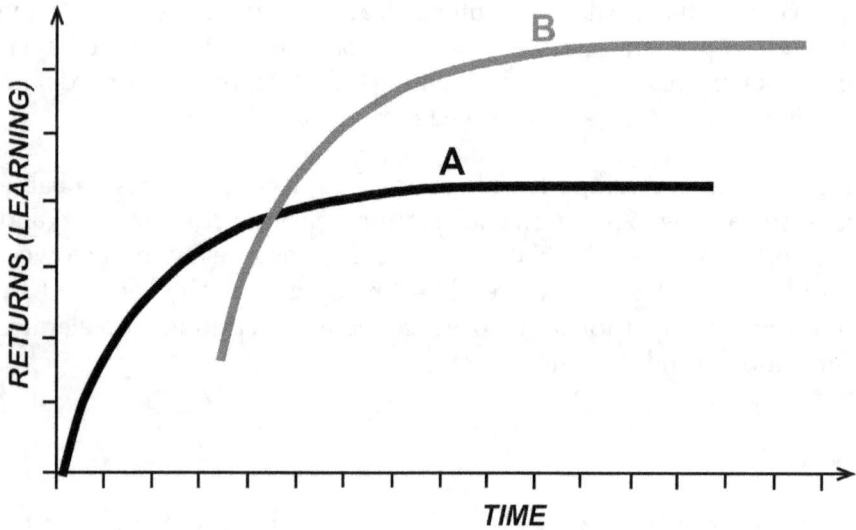

Figure 6.7 New approaches (represented by learning curve B) enable growth after existing approaches (represented by learning curve A) saturate.

Notice that at earlier times returns from learning curve B are lower than learning curve A, which is the reason approach B was not the choice earlier.

The advantage of approach B is it later surpasses approach A. Curves like B, with higher long-term returns, are common when they are based on emerging technologies. Leaders on established learning curves sometimes ignore alternate approaches until competitors pursuing such approaches start impacting their business. Unfortunately, by that time competitors will have the learning advantage in the new approach.

Thus, exploration and innovation (pursuit of next generation learning curves) are important for maintaining long-term competitiveness. This is best done when a company has abundant resources – namely, when existing product lines are generating healthy revenues – and not when a company is under attack.

Pioneers on new learning curves are also better positioned to stake legal claims to new intellectual property. Patents and copyright protection of "best methods" make it harder for later competitors to compete, since they will have to utilize lesser methods or pay royalties to the pioneering company.

Of course, there are no guarantees that new approaches (such as B in Fig. 6.7) will surpass existing approaches, since learning curves are projections of learning that has yet to occur. For example, technical problems could cause the new approach B to saturate at a level below the saturation level of approach A. If that were to happen pursuing approach B would have been a bad idea.

New learning curve shapes can be predicted with greater confidence when they are based on established "technology trends". For example, steadily shrinking chip dimensions have enabled the number of electronic functions integrated onto silicon microchips to approximately double every 18 months for more than 50 years (a trend known as Moore's Law). This trend has led to successive generations of faster, lower cost, microchips. Consequently, learning based on this trend is more likely to be realized than learning based on totally new pursuits.

This is also why visionaries are important for growing companies. These are people who excel at seeing underlying technology and business trends to forecast future market directions.

Relation to Information Turns

Learning curves are intimately related to the *information turns* discussed in Chapter 4. Recall "information turns" are experiments followed by analyses to extract new learning. Exploring new situations is equivalent to performing information turns. In fact, each increment of learning can be viewed as an information turn.

Initial information turns are usually short, as there is much to learn and it is easy to find new information. Subsequent information turns tend to become progressively longer, reflecting the fact the easier methods of finding information have already been used. In our gold mining example, the miner initially needed only to glance around to find gold. Later he had to extract and sift through enormous amounts of material to find gold. Figure 6.8 shows how learning curves relate to information turns. Notice that learning flattens out over time because each increment of learning is taking longer and longer.

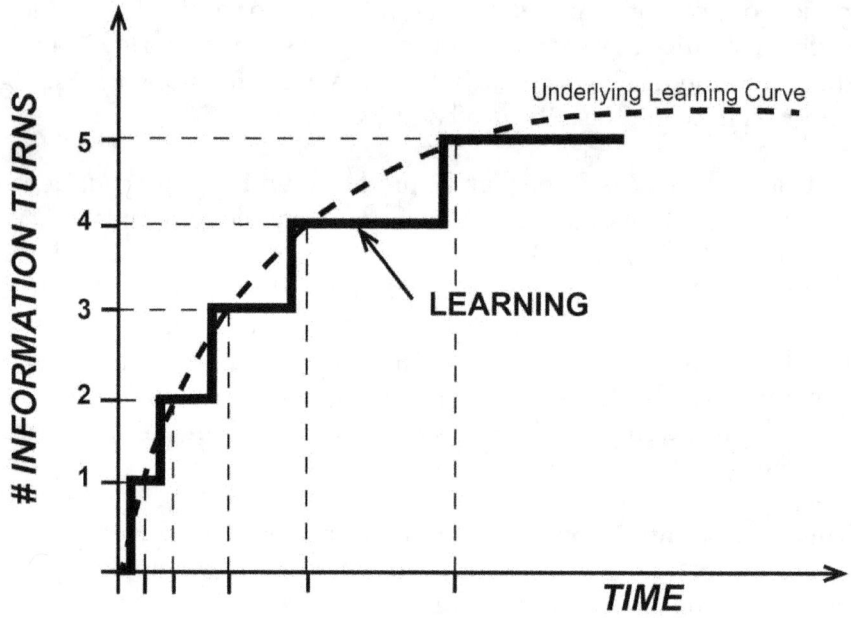

Figure 6.8 Learning curve with information-turns as the unit of learning.

The time to perform an information turn depends on the activity. As we mentioned in Chapter 5, information turns for pharmaceutical developments are often measured in years, whereas information turns in software developments are typically measured in days. Since all learning curves saturate, their lifetimes can differ greatly depending on the activity. For example, developments utilizing new computer models tend to saturate quickly, as information turns can be as short as a few seconds – the time it takes to run a computer simulation. In these situations the limitations of new models are quickly reached, and saturation occurs quickly. Consequently, new and improved models are constantly needed.

Conversely, when the information turns are long, progress down a learning curve will be slow and the lifetime of the learning curve will be long. Biological experiments are in this class, as information turns usually involve controlled testing of groups of animal and human subjects over extended periods of time.

In business, progress is driven by many different information turns – each with potentially widely varying execution times. This raises an obvious question: which information turns determine overall progress? The answer is *the information turns that produce the most learning will be the primary determinant of progress.* Such information turns are referred to as the "technology drivers" for an endeavor.

In digital electronics, the primary technology driver has been computer chip scaling (shrinking of computer chip dimensions). Advances in this area have enabled microchips to be increasingly powerful, energy-efficient, and less expensive. This has led to corresponding advances in computers, digital cameras, mobile phones, automobiles, smart appliances, etc. In short, chip-scaling learning curves have spawned many other learning curves capitalizing on microchip advances.

Manufacturing Learning Curves

Learning curves are also applicable to manufacturing. Each manufactured unit represents an information turn (i.e., an experiment) that provides process learning that can be used to improve the manufacturing process. Process learning includes the discovery of inefficiencies, defects, shortcuts, and improvements during the ramp up of manufacturing. This type of learning is usually unpublished and not in the public domain and maintained as "trade secrets" by the manufacturer. An example of defect learning is shown in Fig. 6.9 below:

Figure 6.9 Example of defects discovered during manufacturing.

Small improvements are easier to find when the number of manufactured units grows. This is because their effects are more easily seen when random variations are averaged out of the data.

For example, in semiconductor chip manufacturing large variations in chip characteristics are common in new processes. Such variations make incremental improvements to the process difficult, since the effects of small changes are masked by random manufacturing variations. However, as the number of manufactured chips grows, the effect of random variations can be averaged out of the data (see Fig 6.10 below). This allows engineers to fine-tune the manufacturing process to lower costs. This is fortuitous, as learning curves also predict improvements will be increasingly small as processes mature. This shows why large manufacturers have an advantage over small manufacturers.

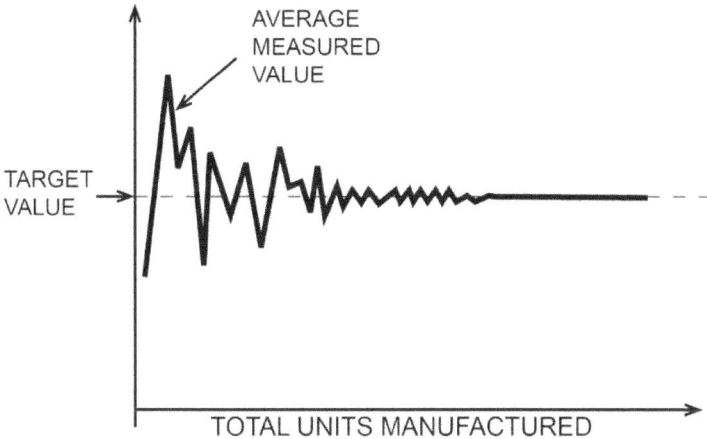

Figure 6.10   Random variations make it difficult to see the effect of small adjustments in manufacturing variables. As volume grows, random variations can be averaged out, making process optimization easier.

Like in all learning curves, for a given manufacturing process new learning eventually levels off and additional improvements result in diminishing returns. The result is the familiar learning curve versus time shape shown in Fig 6.11 where the number of units manufactured is used in place of the time scale.

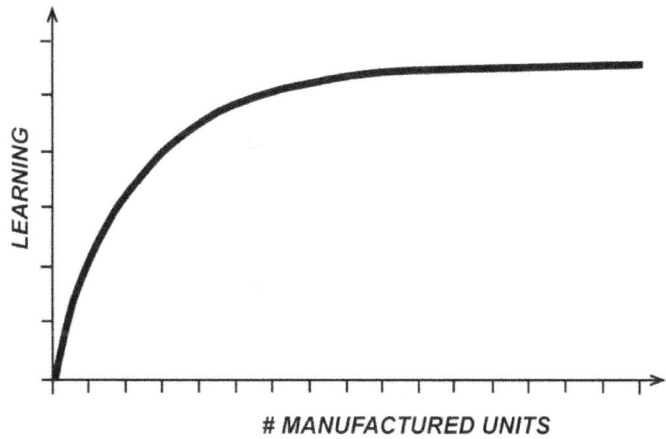

Figure 6.11   Manufacturing learning curve, where units replace time in the horizontal axis.

Manufacturing learning also show why companies that have contracted manufacturing to external vendors (domestic or foreign) may be at a disadvantage when they try to bring manufacturing back into the parent company. Learning gained by the contract manufacturer is often not passed back to the customer, leaving the customer company at a manufacturing disadvantage.

Just as there are technology drivers, there are also *volume drivers* driving progress. For a given level of technology maturity, higher volume products can be improved faster than low volume products because of the greater learning. For example, improvements to personal computers (PC's) occurred at a far faster rate than the older computers they replaced (minicomputers, mainframes) due to their greater volumes. This enabled PC capabilities to advance faster than conventional computers, which further expanded their markets.

More recently, mobile devices (e.g., smartphones, smart watches, etc.) have replaced personal computers as the volume driver, resulting in far greater year-to-year improvements there than in PC's.

Constructive Versus Destructive Learning

Vibrant companies regularly expand their markets to avoid pursuing aging products on maturing learning curves. The key to doing this is exploration of new areas. What is learned, however, depends on the eye of the beholder. Learning can be constructive or destructive.

It can be destructive when negative outcomes cause organizations to abandon broad areas of solution space. In battle terms, this is analogous to retreating from the broad field after a defeat in a local skirmish. An example would be a company whose first product in the mobile communications market is a commercial failure and abandons that market in response.

Since initial products are often unsuccessful, this can cause a company to progressively withdraw from new markets. Adopting this tactic every time problems are encountered will cause a company to steadily shrink its solution space and business. Rather than retreating, it would be better to analyze negative results and understand why an approach failed. Doing so provides information on what changes are needed to succeed. This might include expanding the solution space if the needed modifications cannot be found in the existing space.

This is illustrated in the situation depicted in Fig. 6.12, where a person lost in the wilderness is attempting to light a fire to attract rescue aircraft. In the upper diagram (situation-a) the person searches for fuel only in his immediate surroundings and lights a fire using the few twigs he has found. He discovers the fire is dim and short-lived and resigns himself to not having a fire (retreating by shrinking the solution space). In contrast, the person in the lower diagram (situation-b) searches over a larger area (expanding the solution space) to locate firewood for a much larger fire, greatly improving his chances for rescue.

Figure 6.12   Why expanding the solution space is useful when encountering problems.

Although expanding the solution space in approach-b may seem obvious, it can be a difficult to do. Some people treat negative results as personal failures - not learning experiences.   To avoid such unpleasantness, they may avoid those areas in the future (i.e., retreat). Unfortunately, shrinking the solution space decreases the probability of success.

Managers need to stress that information turns are for learning and foster a culture where learning comes from both positive *and* negative outcomes. In fact, there is often more new information (i.e., more learning) from negative outcomes, especially when the results are unexpected. Few solutions work perfectly the first time, and most project solutions are developed incrementally through a series of positive and negative experiments.

Eating Ones Young

One method for keeping ahead of learning curves is for companies to constantly innovate and replace profitable products with improved products - even if the new products are less profitable initially. Such companies know gains from any given product strategy decline over time, and that products based on new learning curves will eventually supplant current products. Replacing one's own products before another company replaces them is a way to maintain market leadership.

One might question whether this is wise, since another company might still take the lead by pursuing an even better learning curve. If that were to happen, maybe it would have been better to extract maximum profits from existing products for as long as possible. Unfortunately, this is equivalent to assuming long-term failure.

The company that is the leader in existing products should be in a strong position to lead in next-generation products. That company has established sales and support channels and a better understanding of customer needs. If it has been listening to its customers, it should know more about the shortcomings of current products and what needs to be addressed in future offerings.

The market leader also usually has the resource advantage, with more money for developing improvements. If that same company aggressively innovates, it can extend its competitive advantages into next generation products. In the past, companies like Apple and Intel have successfully followed strategies where they routinely obsoleted their own products to maintain long-term market leadership.

Summary

All business processes are governed by learning curves, where learning and benefits from a business approach decline over time. Managers need to monitor process trends to predict when existing learning curves are going to saturate, and work with visionaries to identify next generation learning curves to pursue.

Learning curve lifetimes vary greatly. Faster information turns result in shorter lifetime learning curves.

Learning curves have special implications in manufacturing and show why it is difficult to compete against established manufacturers by simply copying their processes.

Finally, learning and progress usually occur incrementally. Learning is derived from both negative and positive information turns. It is important that negative results not lead to broad retreats, otherwise transitions to new learning curves may occur too late.

Learning curves mean every product strategy has a finite lifetime. Companies that understand their learning curves are better able to stay competitive over the long term.

7. Focus, Metrics, & Models

Importance of Focus

Lack of focus is a problem in many businesses. Overly general objectives and goals are symptoms of this problem. Broad objectives are good for describing the mission of an organization, but are inadequate for defining actionable strategies. Specific goals and plans are needed to keep an organization from going off in too many directions.

Defining focused goals and execution strategies are among the more challenging jobs of management. The challenge stems from uncertainties inherent in all management actions - namely, that it is impossible to predict the exact consequences of any management action. The best one can do is predict the probable result. This causes some managers to keep multiple options on the table and not focus on specific strategies.

Unfortunately, lack of focus lessens the likelihood of achieving business objectives, as it disperses resources in directions not contributing to project goals (see Fig. 7.1). While there is risk in all execution strategies, the risks are not equal. Focusing resources on the lowest risk strategies (i.e., the strategies most likely to succeed) maximizes chances for success. Organizations are more efficient when its members have clear directions and concrete goals.

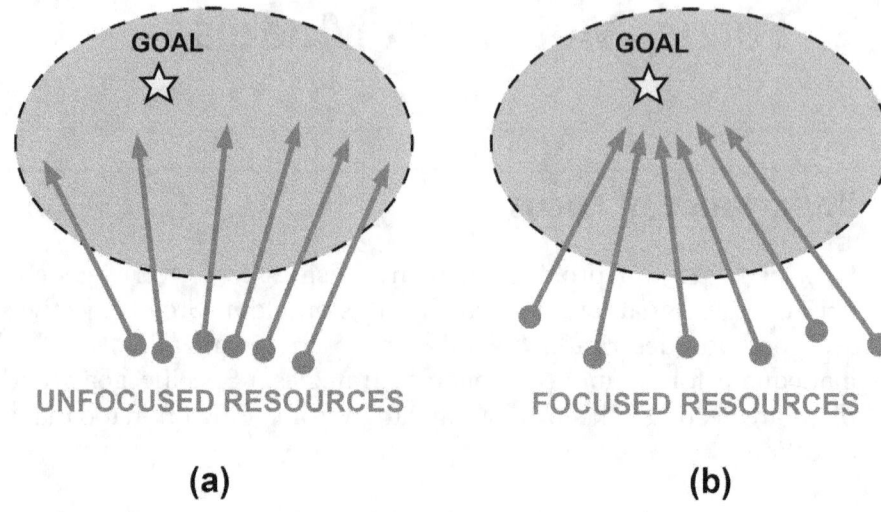

Figure 7.1 Lack of focus (a) causes limited resources to be spread across pursuits not contributing to project success.

Having clear, well-defined project goals focuses employee energies. Providing this organizational focus is one of the jobs of management.

Restricting the solution space for employees is one way of providing focus. For example, the "solution space" for a new microchip design could be restricted by setting limits on manufacturing cost, power dissipation, performance, and delivery schedule.   Too large a solution space wastes resources by allowing workers to pursue unacceptable solutions. Conversely, too small a solution space may not yield a solution. Analysis and judgment are needed to define solution spaces that can accomplish goals efficiently (see Fig. 7.2).

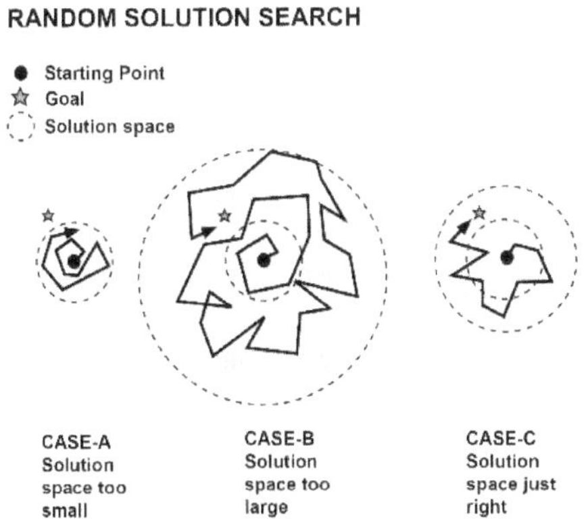

RANDOM SOLUTION SEARCH

● Starting Point
☆ Goal
◌ Solution space

CASE-A
Solution
space too
small

CASE-B
Solution
space too
large

CASE-C
Solution
space just
right

Figure 7.2 Comparison of possible solution space sizes: A is too small,
B is too large, and C is just right.

While C may be ideal, it can be difficult to find in practice since we
do not know where the solution is beforehand. It is better to start
with a somewhat too large a solution space rather than too small and
use information from initial searches (early information turns) to
narrow search areas in subsequent solution searches.   This
narrowing process is depicted in Fig. 7.3.

● Starting Point
☆ Goal
◌ Solution space

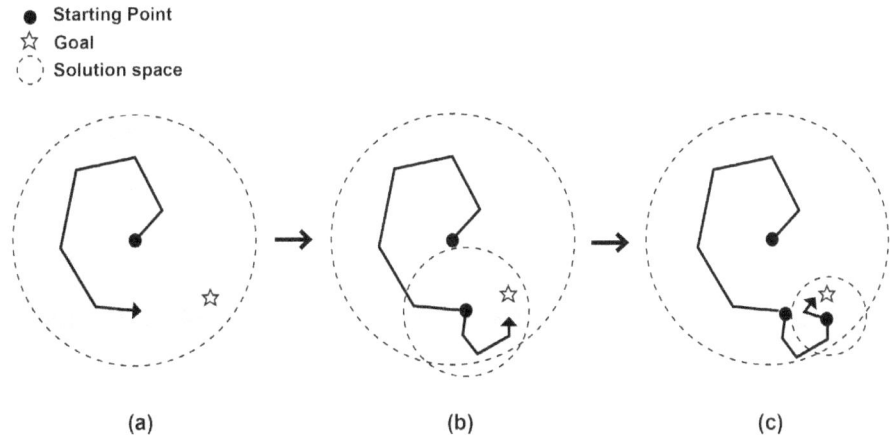

(a)   (b)   (c)

Figure 7.3 An initial wide search (a) can help exclude areas where
solutions are unlikely. This enables subsequent searches to focus on areas
more likely to contain solutions (the shaded areas in b and c).

Note that enlarging a solution space is equivalent to relaxing the boundary conditions for solutions. For example, the original solution space for a consumer product might have set the maximum manufacturing cost at $10.00 per unit. If developers later found this was unachievable, management might choose to increase the target to $15.00 per unit. Doing so changes the boundary conditions for solution, expanding manufacturing options. However, raising product cost *reduces* the solution space for marketing and sales. Again, it is management's job to balance such tradeoffs and assess whether revised plans still meet project objectives.

Use of Metrics

A particularly useful tool for providing focus is the adoption of *metrics* or quantitative indicators of progress. Metrics are measurables that correlate with project progress. Their purpose is to provide a convenient means for monitoring progress.

The popularity of metrics has grown greatly in past years with the growth of "continuous improvement" programs (programs aimed at steady incremental improvements). When accurate, metrics can be used to measure the effectiveness of incremental changes as well as provide targets for interim goals.

The management challenge is identifying metrics that accurately correlate with progress. While it is easy to find metrics that mostly correlate with progress, it is far more difficult to find metrics that *always* correlate with progress.

A metric that increases for most actions *towards* goals, but also for some actions *away* from goals, can be misleading. For example, one might think the number of calls per month to a customer support line would be a good metric for measuring the quality of a software product. It seems logical that higher quality software would require fewer calls for assistance. If this metric were used as the sole measure of product quality the results could be misleading. For example, if product problems were growing in number and complexity, each call would require more time to address customer problems. If all the support personnel were busy, each support person would be spending more time with fewer customers. Other customers seeking help might hang-up after experiencing excessive wait times to speak to a support person. The preceding metric would show fewer calls per month to the support line, suggesting improving quality while it was exactly the opposite. This could lead management to conclude quality was fine and that engineering should focus resources on adding more features (potentially aggravating quality problems).

The previous example shows that metrics need to be defined carefully and used judiciously. If not, they can cause organizations to go in wrong directions. In some situations, several metrics may be needed to obtain an accurate measure of progress. Once again management judgment plays major roles – both in selecting the metrics and defining procedures for their use.

For most businesses there are some obvious metrics to be tracked. They include cash flow (e.g., monthly revenue minus monthly expenditures) and number of customers. For businesses providing professional services, the number of billable hours per month is another common metric.

The explosion of web-based advertising is partially due to the availability of excellent metrics. The numbers of people visiting a web site and making purchases there is easily measured, making it easy to gauge the effectiveness of such advertising.

Good metrics are especially useful in large, complex organizations – especially ones with many levels of management (see Fig. 7.4).

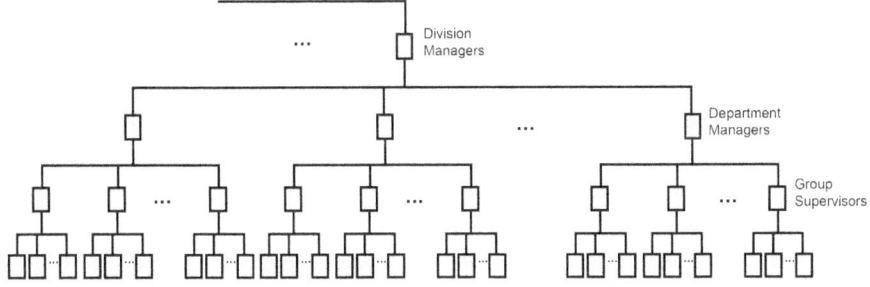

Figure 7.4 Typical management hierarchy in a large organization.

In large organizations, multiple levels of management are used to keep the number of people reporting directly to each manager to manageable levels. However, such hierarchies separate higher-level managers from the employees who are performing the actual work (the ones at the bottom). Communication through intermediate managers requires information to be reinterpreted and retransmitted at multiple levels. This can lead to delays and errors in interpretation, errors that may be magnified at successive levels of transmission.

Good metrics, on the other hand, are less prone to such errors since they can bypass the management hierarchy and flow directly to each management level. Fig, 7.5 compares information flowing through direct reports versus through metrics.

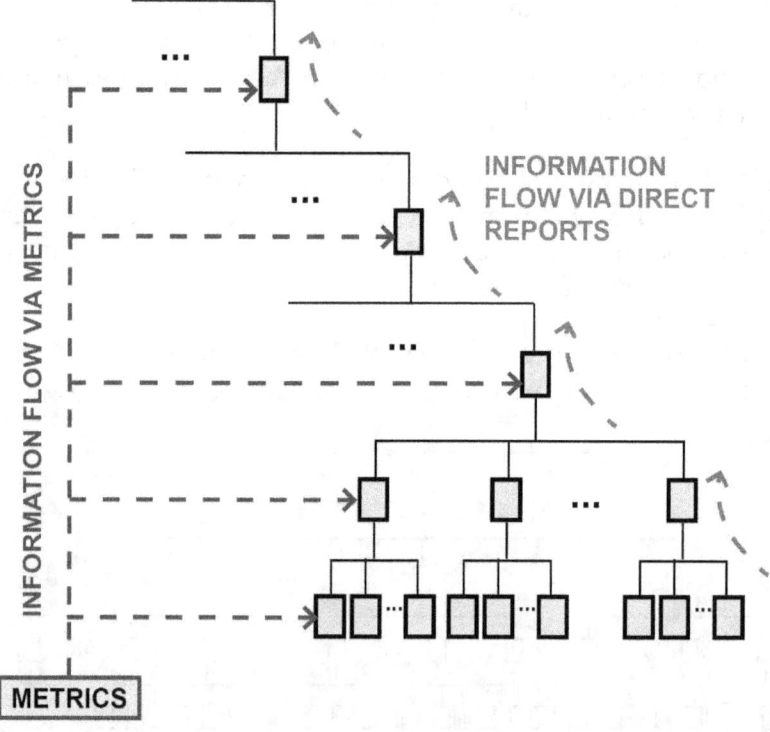

Figure 7.5 Unlike information via direct reports, information from metrics is available at all levels of management without reinterpretation.

Models

Metrics are especially useful when their relationship to project variables can be represented by *mathematical models*. For example, in microchip engineering, mathematical models of electronic circuits can predict performance and power consumption metrics of various designs before physical circuits are built. Such models allow engineers and managers to explore different designs before committing them to manufacturing. Models allow "what-if" analyses to be performed rapidly on a computer, enabling many different designs to be evaluated at low cost. This allows for a much broader exploration of options than would be possible through experimental testing of physical circuits.

Formal business plans are a form of models (see our discussions in Chapter 5). Business plans are structured documents that combine information about a company's proposed products and services, competitor analysis, target customers, and marketing plans to create a quantitative model of cash flow. Such models are useful for entrepreneurs as they can be used to maximize the likelihood of business success.   Provided entrepreneurs have done their homework in providing accurate inputs to such plans, the resulting cash flow projections are models that can serve as "what if" tools for evaluating different business scenarios. For example, the benefits of different pricing and volume strategies could be compared. Although the predicted "best" scenario will only be as good as the assumptions in the business model, it will still be the "best guess" given available information. As we have said repeatedly, it is advantageous to launch a business using the best scenario rather than the third or fourth best scenario.

The accuracy of any model can be significantly improved if they are adjusted to match existing data (see Fig. 7.6). This "calibration process" compensates for deficiencies in the models – especially for models that can accurately predict trends but not absolute values. Such models can be used to "extend" information beyond existing data.

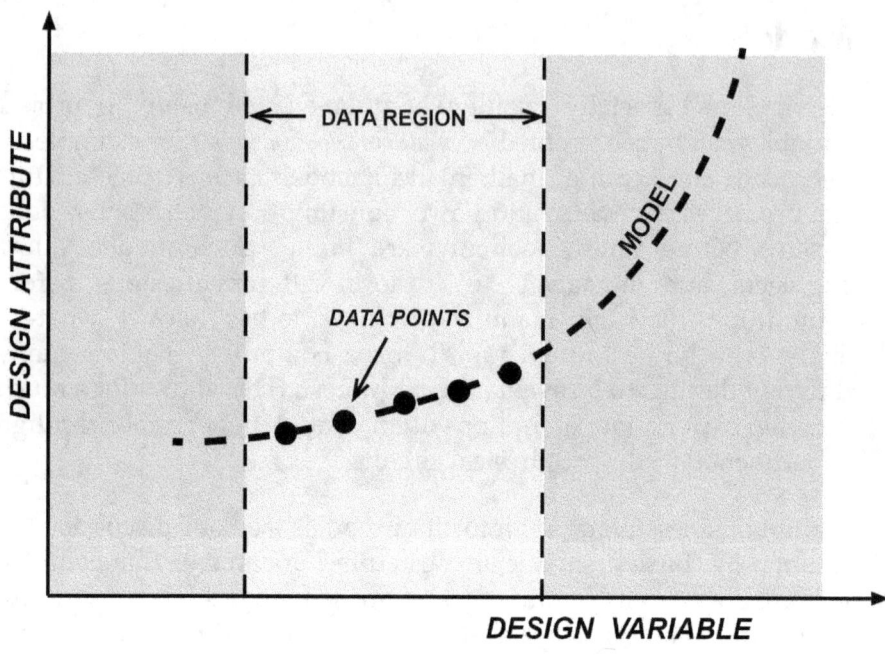

Figure 7.6 How a model (the dotted curve) can be used to predict behavior outside the data region.

Solution Optimization

One of the more powerful uses of metric models is *solution optimization*. The optimum solution is the one that accomplishes project objectives using the least amount of resources. Accurate metric models can be used to find optimum solutions.

For example, microchip metric models can be used to automatically find the lowest-power circuit designs meeting speed targets.

Another application example would be using metric models to compare internal versus subcontracted product manufacturing. Metrics for factory setup costs, unit manufacturing costs versus volume, etc., could be entered into a financial model to predict the sales volume for which internal manufacturing is more cost effective than subcontracted manufacturing.

Model-Driven Solution Development

Models can also steer experiments (information turns) to accelerate solution development. When models calibrated with prior data are refined with new data, the recalibrated models can be used to point to next solution steps and experiments. If this process is performed repeatedly, the refined models become repositories of accumulated learning.

A flow diagram illustrating the basic methodology is shown in Fig. 7.7 below.

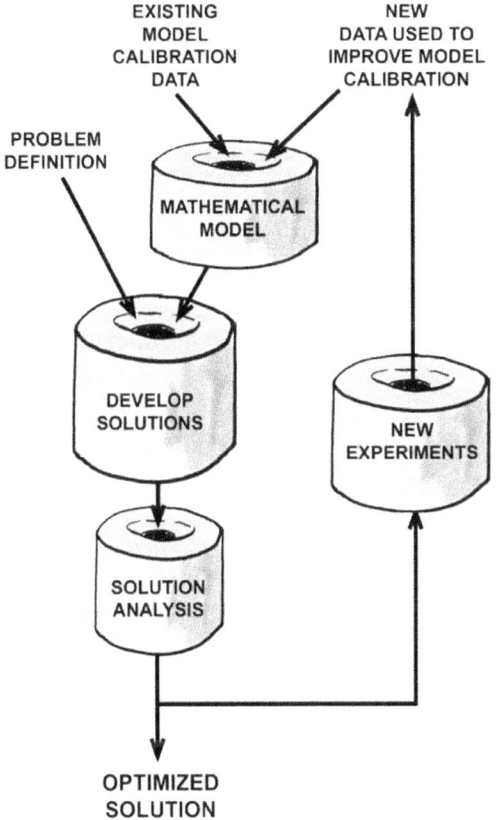

Figure 7.7 The role of models in solution development

In Fig. 7.7 models are used to predict directions for the next increment of progress. Experiments are performed to validate predictions. If the experiments match the models, the same models are used to predict further directions of progress. When experiments show model predictions deviating from experiments, the models are refined (i.e., recalibrated) to fit both new and previous data before being used to predict the next increment of progress. This process continues iteratively to progress towards the final solution. Model-driven processes like these enable solutions to be found more quickly than with experiments alone.

In this process the models and experiments are working in partnership: where models define next experiments and the results from those experiments refine models. Such models not only serve as repositories of accumulated learning, they provide managers with increasingly accurate tools for engineering.

Artificial Intelligence Models

A more recent trend is the development of *Artificial Intelligence (AI) computer models*, which model effects and behavior using massive amounts of information rather than mathematical algorithms.

The algorithm-based models discussed earlier were calibrated to match available data to compensate for phenomena not explicitly modeled. In contrast, AI models do not need an underlying algorithmic model, but instead utilize large amounts of data to both *create and calibrate* models.

AI models capture effects in a manner analogous to the way human brains learn when exposed to different experiences. "Neural net circuits" in AI models mimic the behavior of neurons in human brains by altering their properties based on the information they are fed. The resulting "machine learning" allow such models to replicate the behavior imbedded in the learning information.

Such AI models have several attractions. First, *they do not require detailed understanding of mechanisms*, and are thus easily created when large amounts of empirical data are available. Second, *the resulting AI models execute extremely quickly*, since the neural net circuitry in such models do not require the complex mathematical calculations of algorithmic models. As such, AI models are especially useful in applications requiring rapid, real-time predictions, such as those in production line screening, self-driving automobiles, automated camera systems, etc. Such models are also attractive for activities too complex to model algorithmically, such as medical diagnoses.

The limitation of such models is they are less useful for detailed predictions or fine optimization, since they lack algorithmic modeling of detailed effects. As a consequence, AI model predictions are not always precise or accurate, since they only reflect the behavior of the data used to calibrate them. There are, however, many applications where being 90% correct is sufficient. Furthermore, AI models can also learn from predictions made by algorithmic models. A combination of AI models and algorithmic models can be the optimum solution for many applications.

Summary

Focus is paramount for efficient utilization of resources. The areas for focus need to be specified carefully - to ensure they are neither too broad nor overly narrow. Quantitative measures of progress, or metrics, can aid focus when they are defined carefully. Poor metrics, however, can lead projects astray.

Mathematical modeling of metrics can be especially useful. When accurate, such models can accelerate solution prediction and optimization. They are particularly useful when utilized in partnership with information turns (experiments).

Artificial Intelligence (AI) models take direct advantage of available information and can provide fast models of complex effects.

8. Balancing Reward & Risk

Since all management plans have uncertainties, every management decision contains some risk of failure. This means every decision is a gamble, one which the decision-maker hopes are correct and contributes to success. For a manager, a key task is judging whether the risks are worthwhile.

Statistical Odds

Let me illustrate the problem using the casino roulette wheel shown in Fig. 8.1. The wheel can stop at any of 30 positions. The house's rule for play is as follows: if a spin of the wheel stops at a player's position, the house will give $20 for each $1 a player bets on that position. If wheel fails to land on a player's position, the house takes all the money bet on that position.

Step right up folks, pick your number and place your bets.
Get **20X** your money when the wheel stops at your number!!

Figure 8.1 Roulette wheel example

The question is what are the odds a player will come out ahead in this game? In this case, it is easy to calculate. Since the roulette wheel has 30 positions, the likelihood of it landing on a specific position in any spin is 1/30. This means an average of 30 tries will be needed to obtain a win on a specific position. If the player bets $1 for each try, he or she will on average have spent $30 for each win. Since each win only nets the player $20, the player will lose to the house if the player plays long enough. Of course, no one participating in such games believes it will take 30 tries to win. Most hope they will be lucky and win in the first few tries. The odds are against that, however, and it is possible that one may not win in over 60 tries.

But what if the house's position is to pay out $40 for each $1 bet? The chance of it landing on the player's position is still 1/30, meaning on average it will still take 30 tries (or $30) for each win, but since each win is $40, the player will come out of ahead if he or she plays long enough. Alternatively, if the player is only willing to try 10 spins, the chances of winning are only 10/30 = 0.3 or 30%, which is still low. The house, on the other hand, will lose money over the long term with such a payout, as many people will play that same wheel and over time more money will be paid out than taken in.

Reward/Risk Ratio

We can gauge the odds by examining the ratio of reward versus risk:

$$\text{REWARD/RISK} = \frac{\text{REWARD (Gain from success)}}{\text{RISK (Total cost, incl. cost of failures)}}$$

Unless one is counting on being especially lucky, this ratio needs to be greater than one to come out ahead over the long term.

PROJECT   **REWARDS**
EXPENSES   **FROM SUCCESS**

Figure 8.2   Significance of the Reward/Risk formula is depicted above. It means balancing risk versus rewards.

Managers need to perform a similar evaluation of the rewards and risks in their projects.

Although the calculation of Reward/Risk is more complicated for projects than for the preceding roulette wheel, equivalent evaluations are needed if an organization is to be successful over the long term. To make business sense, this ratio needs to be greater than one – ideally, much more than one.

Venture capitalists know this when they are investing money in startup companies. It is difficult to forecast the success of immature technologies since markets and competition have yet to develop. Consequently, the risk of failure in startups is high. For example, it is not unusual for venture firms to back startups whose likelihood of success is only 20%. Venture firms, however, back many companies. If they back five companies in different areas, each with a 20% chance if success, it is likely one of those companies will be successful. Applying the statistical concepts discussed in chapter 4, the likelihood of all 5 companies failing is $(1 - 0.2) \times (1 - 0.2) \times (1 - 0.2) \times (1 - 0.2) \times (1 - 0.2) = .33$ or 33%, meaning there is a 67% chance of one or more companies succeeding. If the gain from a single success is sufficiently large, the Reward/Risk ratio of the Venture firm's portfolio can still be greater than 1 even if 4 of 5 backed companies fail.

This is why venture firms are only interested in companies that promise large payouts if they are successful. The gains from the successes must be enough to compensate for losses from the failures.

Note that if the company were to only back three companies the odds worsen. The probability of all three companies failing is 51%, meaning the likelihood of a success is only 49%.

Reward/Risk Ratio for Projects

These same considerations need to be applied to any project where there is a significant risk of failure.

High risk projects include those with aggressive goals and those directed at long-range needs. Such projects have large uncertainties and thus high risks. To make business sense, the reward from success must be large enough to compensate for the likely failures (i.e., the number of project iterations needed to achieve success).

This is particularly important for long-range projects, where unforeseen problems are likely. Goals need to be aggressive in such projects to ensure results will be competitive at the future delivery date. Many information turns and project iterations will probably be needed to achieve goals. Project plans need to account for the time and cost of those iterations. More important, the rewards from project success need to be commensurate with the costs. Specifically, the Reward/Risk ratio needs to be much greater than one to make business sense.

Note that the numerator in the Reward/Risk formula is the *total* gain, including indirect benefits. For example, while profits from direct sales of a new product might be modest, the total gain could be larger if one includes the marketing value from establishing an image of technology leadership.

Note that The Reward/Risk ratio of most projects will be low initially, since it takes time to accrue benefits (profit from the sale of a new product). This is depicted in Fig. 8.3 below, which shows the actual Reward/Risk ratio not exceeding one until after some later time, t1.

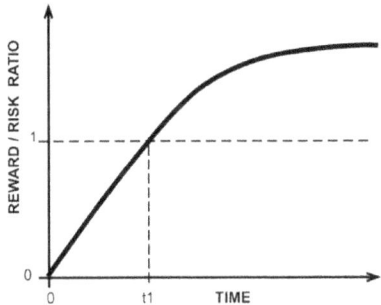

Figure 8.3 Graph of Reward/Risk over time.

Notice that the long-term Reward/Risk ratio flattens out as the product matures (from saturation of its learning curve). For business planning, the Reward/Risk at the projected lifetime of the product is used to evaluate whether the projected Reward/Risk is sufficient. In other words, the accumulated gain to the company is the Reward to be used in the Reward/Risk formula.

The bigger challenge is how to calculate the denominator in the Reward/Risk ratio - as failures are never intended nor planned. A combination of management judgment and statistical analysis can be used to estimate this. Managers can combine their experience with similar projects plus their knowledge of resources (e.g., the abilities of their staff) to estimate the likelihood of success of different solution approaches (e.g., 25%, 50%, 75%, or 90%, ...). Such numbers can be used to estimate the likely number solution iterations (i.e., failures) to achieve success. For example, if the likelihood of success is 50%, the estimated cost of the information turns in a development plan needs to be doubled to account for the two iterations. Likewise, if the likelihood of success is only 25%, four iterations are likely needed before success.

Mathematically speaking, such analyses are statistically correct only if each attempt is independent of every other attempt and each had similar probabilities of failure. In practice, succeeding project attempts will use learning gained in earlier attempts and not be independent. Nevertheless, such analyses are still useful for estimating development costs for planning purposes. Since we cannot know in advance how an approach might fail or what learning might be gained, such estimates may be the *best* that can be made during the planning phase. Such analyses are thus useful for evaluating the relative odds of different approaches and judging whether project cost is commensurate with goals.

Role of Focus

It is also important to stay focused on project goals when estimating Reward/Risk ratios. There are activities where Reward/Risk ratios might be large if measured against long-range goals, but small for the goals of the project at hand. Let me illustrate this with an example from the semiconductor industry.

Suppose the project is to develop an industry-leading computer chip manufacturing process in two years. Consider two different approaches for tackling that goal: in (a) engineers improve basic understanding of fundamental microchip mechanisms and use that understanding to develop physics-based computer models for engineering the process, versus (b) where engineers use existing computer models to extrapolate experimental data and make local predictions for engineering the process. These two approaches are contrasted in Fig. 8.4 below.

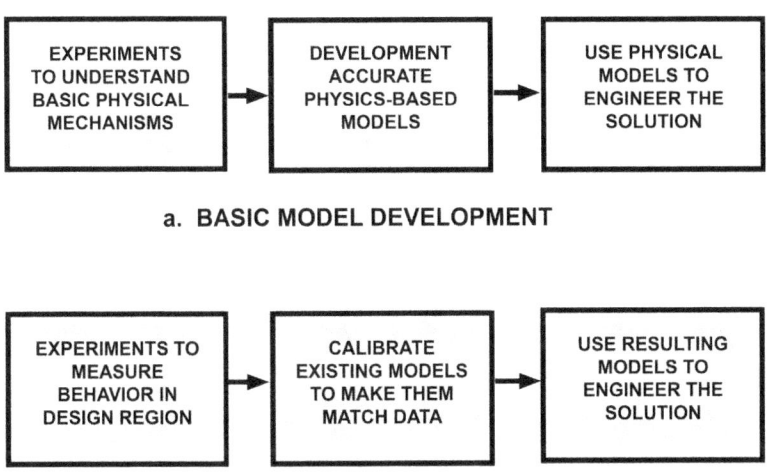

a. BASIC MODEL DEVELOPMENT

b. TAILORED MODEL DEVELOPMENT

Figure 8.4 Two different approaches for developing a next generation computer chip manufacturing process. In (a) the focus is on improving the predictive accuracy of general physics-based models. In (b) the focus is on calibrating existing models for the specific project.

Approach-a is conceptually attractive, since it promises deeper understanding of basic mechanisms, allowing development of more optimized solutions for project goals. It also provides models that will be more useful for future projects. However, modern chip technologies are exceedingly complex, and physical phenomena in many critical paths are poorly understood. It is unlikely understanding could be improved enough in the timeframe of this project to create general modeling tools accurate enough for its needs.

In contrast, Approach-b can be applied to all project critical paths for which there is data. The availability of such data is usually not a problem, as planners normally focus on solution paths supported by experimental data. By forcing available models to match available data, unknown phenomena are compensated for in the calibration.

The resulting models can then be used to make predictions beyond existing data. Such models are always easier and faster to develop than the general models in Approach-a.

Since Approach-b has lower risk, it is the one with a higher Reward/Risk ratio for this project. The fundamental research approach expounded in Approach-a is more appropriate for a long-range research program to build basic knowledge and understanding - a *different* project than the project at hand, one with a much longer time frame. Such projects are better suited for universities and research consortiums, where costs are shared, and the output are publications in technical journals. In general, it is better to not mix long-range project objectives with short-term project goals.

"Quick, take the baton!!" "I have to finish my exercises."

Figure 8.5 Mixing short and long-term priorities can hurt project success.

In terms of the bigger picture, there is a symbiotic relationship between Approach-a and Approach-b. Existing physical models in Approach-a serve as the starting point for the models used for the calibrations in Approach-b. As models in Approach-b are applied far beyond their calibration points, predictions will eventually deviate from measurements due to limitations in the models. Such mismatches provide information aiding development of improved models in Approach-a. This synergy between the Approach-a and Approach-b is depicted in Fig. 8.6 below.

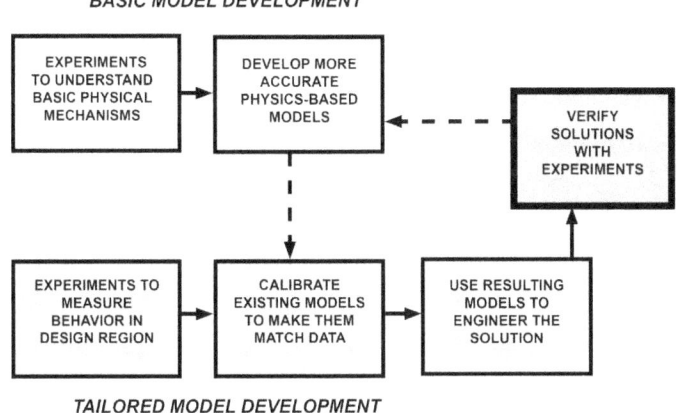

Figure 8.6 Synergy between basic models and tailored models.

As always, there are exceptions to every rule. For example, if progress in a chip manufacturing project were to be gated by critical paths with excellent existing physical models (e.g., lithography resolution), extending models in that area might be the fastest way of achieving project objectives. As always, management judgment is needed when applying any of these concepts.

Being Lucky versus Smart

Given this chapter is about risk taking, it seems appropriate to pose the age-old question: is it better to be lucky than smart? "Lucky" means succeeding despite statistical odds to the contrary.

The odds of winning lottery raffles are extremely small, yet millions of people regularly purchase lottery tickets for a chance to be a winner. People reason someone will win, so why not them? Buying multiple tickets and participating in many raffles increases one's chances of winning, but the likelihood is still small. Yet it is true that someone always wins, so someone will be "lucky".

There are high-risk activities where luck is needed. As we mentioned previously, it is okay to pursue such activities if the rewards from an eventual success are large enough to compensate for likely failures. In the case of lotteries, the risk-reward ratio is always less than one since lotteries are designed to take in more money (from ticket sales) than they give out (through awards). One could guarantee winning by buying all the lottery tickets, but the awards would be less than the cost of all the tickets.

So, if we are relying on luck what role does being smart play? The answer is it plays a big role. Careful analyses of available plans can ensure we are picking the least risky approach. The amount of luck required depends on the statistical probability of success – the smaller the probability of success, the greater the amount of luck needed. Using analyses to maximize that probability of success decreases the amount of luck needed and *increase* the chances of being lucky. In short, being smart makes it easier to be lucky. The reason for this is illustrated in the diagram in Fig. 8.7, which shows probability curves depicting the speed distributions for two different design approaches, A & B. Bell-shaped probability curves like those shown are typical when variations in product performance are due to random variations in manufacturing.

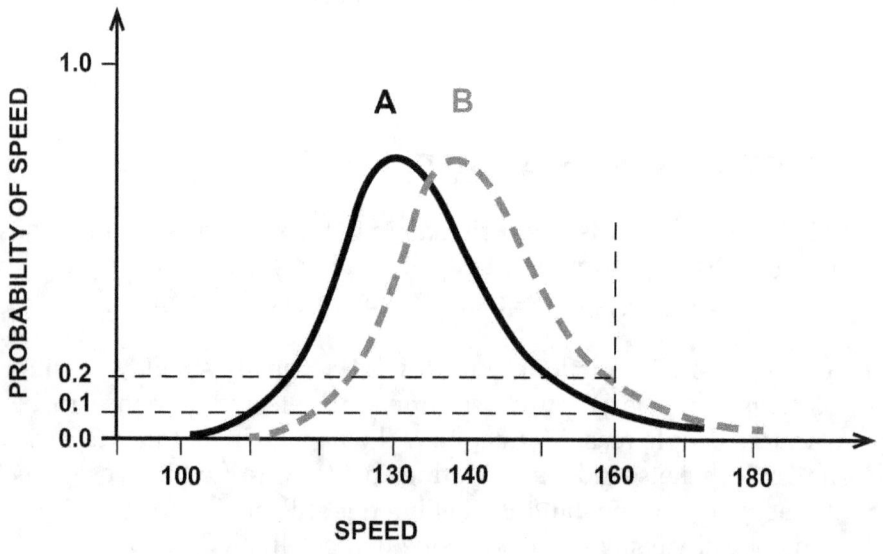

Figure 8.7 Probability curves for slightly different approaches.

Suppose we find customers are willing to pay a significant premium for product at speeds 160 and above. In Curve A only 0.1 or 10% of the product are at that speed, whereas 0.2 or 20% of the product in B are at that speed, twice that of A. In both approaches only a small fraction of the manufactured product is premium, but there is twice as much premium product in B than in A. Thus, it is much easier to be lucky in solution B than A.

Even though the two approaches differ only slightly, the exponential nature of bell-shaped probability curves result in significant differences in the tails of the curves – multiplying the "luck" factor. This points out that even when the statistical odds are poor, the odds can vary greatly for different solutions.

Knowledge is key to identifying the better solutions. It is not an accident that some people are routinely "luckier" than others. They not only take more risks and explore new areas, but they also use the knowledge gained from failures to increase their chances of success in subsequent attempts. This is the reason many successful entrepreneurs have a long history of risk taking, and why they have failed many times before succeeding.

Fig. 8.8 Which of these divers is more prepared for luck?

In other words, being "smart" increases one's chances of being lucky.

Summary

All management plans have uncertainties, meaning all are at some risk of failure. The degree of risk needs to be incorporated into project planning processes, with time and resources allocated for likely failures. The cost of the failures needs to be included in the planning and balanced against expected benefits from the project.

Finally, while luck is always a factor in success, the chances of being lucky increases when one uses available information to maximize the probability of success.

9. Management Leverage

This chapter deals with gauging the benefits of various actions. Different actions produce different benefits. Since the job of management is maximizing project success, picking the best actions are part of the job.

I use the term "**leverage**" to denote *the net benefit from an action for a given expenditure of time and resources*. The net benefit is the sum of all the positive consequences minus all the negative consequences stemming from that action. When comparing two actions, an action is said to have *higher leverage* if it produces more benefits for the same expenditure of time and resources or the same benefits with less time and resources. From the point of view of management, actions with higher leverage are always preferable.

The benefits should also be commensurate with the expenditure of resources and time. For example, it is probably unwise to spend 50% of a project's resources or time to advance a project's progress by only 10%. We are referring to the *progress scale* here, or the proportion of major problems to be completed in the project. This may be different from the *time scale*, where routine tasks might consume much of the schedule time.

Among the more important jobs of management is picking actions that maximize leverage. Fig. 9.1 illustrates how different actions vary in leverage.

a.

b.

Figure 9.1   Fixing a leak while the boat is in dry dock (a) is a higher leverage activity than fixing the leak while at sea (b).

To illustrate the concept of leverage in the business world, consider a common activity: progress reports.   Progress reports are communication tools for keeping management, customers, and partners informed about a project's status. Progress reports issued immediately after problems arise give stakeholders the maximum amount of time to address the problems (i.e., fix the problems and adjust plans). The same progress report issued a week later will be less useful as there will be one week less time for addressing problems. Since the resources and time for preparing early versus late reports are similar, the late report is lower leverage than the early report. Timely reporting is part of good management.

Another business example can be found in presentations. Delivering a training talk to one employee is a lower leverage activity than delivering that same talk to a group of employees. The preparation effort is approximately the same, but the managerial benefit is greater in the second situation.

Managers are major influencers on leverage in their organizations. Management plans determine which actions are taken and management policies define the procedures for carrying out those actions. The environment and infrastructure for executing actions is also determined by management.

The following are some areas where management actions can influence leverage:

Focus

Managers need to ensure project participants know what the primary objectives of their project are. While secondary objectives, such as employee training, future market development, etc., are laudable, they can be distractions if team members are not focused on primary objectives. Unless the primary objectives are clear, members may switch their efforts to easier, secondary objectives when they run into difficulties on primary objectives – reducing focus just when more effort is needed. This not only reduces leverage but adds overhead from switching between multiple tasks (recall our discussions on the inefficiencies of multitasking in Chapter 4).

The consequences from lack of focus are illustrated in Fig. 9.2.

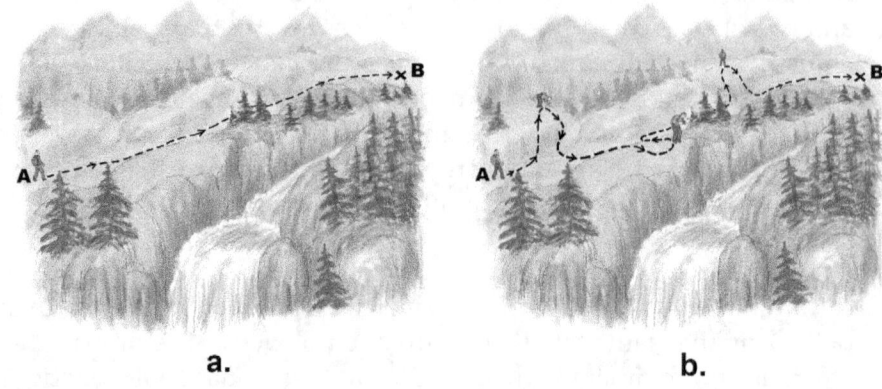

a.   **b.**

Figure 9.2 Focused versus unfocused approaches of getting from A to B.

If the goal of the project in Fig. 9.2 is to go from A to B and locate the gold hidden near B, the person in Case-**b** - who stops to smell flowers, photograph a waterfall, and admire distant mountains – is lower leverage than the person in Case-**a**. Not only will the person in Case-**a** get to B quicker; he or she will also expend less energy in the process.

Synchronization

Leverage also depends on the time when results are generated. In our previous discussion about progress reports we pointed out leverage is greatest when reports are issued promptly. All projects have customers - whether they be internal customers (managers, associates, partners, etc.) or external customers (end-users, distributors, contractors, vendors, etc.). Meeting customer needs means delivering results when needed. Late deliveries disrupt customer plans, reducing project benefits and leverage. A key consideration is *value time*, the value of project results versus delivery time. Value and leverage are greatest when results are *synchronized* with customer plans and expectations.

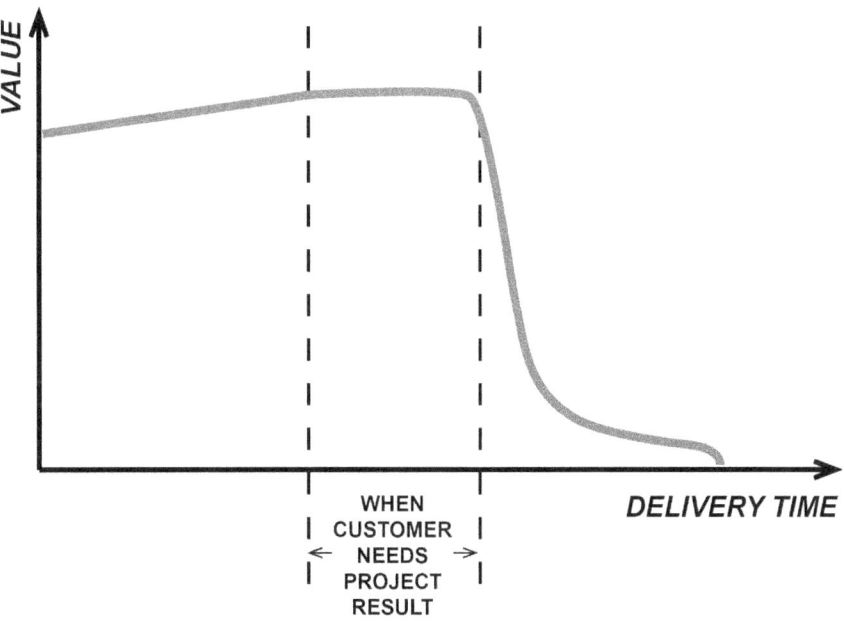

Figure 9.3 Graph illustrating project value versus delivery time.

Fig. 9.3 is a plot show value versus delivery time. Value is greatest when the results are delivered when needed by the customer. If results are delivered later than customer needs its value is greatly reduced (possibly to zero, if the customer no longer wants the result). Its value will also be lower if delivered too early, since the results must be stored, adding overhead costs.

Understanding customer requirements and synchronization windows is important for maximizing leverage.

Communication

Teams of employees, not lone individuals, are typically used to tackle big projects, with activities partitioned among members of the project. However, all plans have uncertainties and unanticipated problems can arise among members. When they do, plans need to be adjusted to maximize the probability of meeting project objectives. This means unexpected problems need to be *communicated promptly* to all participants.

If unanticipated events (e.g., technical difficulties, delivery delays, accidents, etc.) are not promptly communicated, team members will become increasingly unsynchronized, and progress will gradually diverge from plan. It can lead to team members working at cross-purposes - diminishing leverage. Since there are usually more ways for activities to be unsynchronized than synchronized, active management is necessary to keep project activities synchronized.

This is illustrated in Fig. 9.4 below. The three workers, A, B and C, are all focused on the project goal at the start of the project. Unanticipated events cause Worker-B to diverge from plan, delaying that person's intermediate contributions in the plan. Since team members rely on results from others, delays by one team member can lead to delays in other team members, multiplying the number of unanticipated events. The growth of such events will increasingly invalidate the original plan, necessitating major plan corrections. The disruptions will be minimized if corrections to problems are made before their impact spreads to more team members.

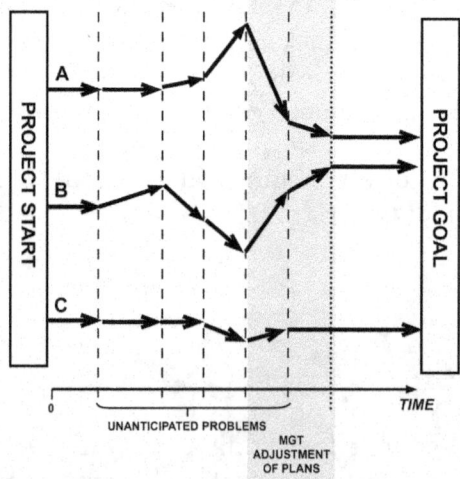

Figure 9.4 Unanticipated events can cause plans to go awry if plans are not adjusted quickly.

Policies and Procedures

Policies and procedures also affect leverage, since they add overhead tasks that consume resources and time. Although formal procedures are needed for efficient operation (e.g., for synchronization, management communication, specifications, etc.), if they are overly bureaucratic they can consume excessive resources and time. When this happens, they lower leverage by using resources that would be better spent on primary objectives.

Figure 9.5 Bureaucratic versus "real" activity.

Keeping policies and procedures to the minimum needed for planning and executing a project maximizes leverage. This is easier with flexible policies and procedures, ones that can be adapted to specific projects, versus a "one size fits all" approach. The latter impose the policies and procedures for the most complex project on the simplest projects, adding unnecessary overhead to simple projects.

Re-Use

Another method for increasing leverage is planning activities so results can be reused in future projects. For example, if a project includes development of user-interface software, developing that software so that major portions of its code can be re-used in future applications will speed future developments. This increases the net benefit from that activity, increasing its leverage. Developing for re-use does incur additional costs, however (additional documentation, adoption of standardized interfaces, etc.), so the benefits must be weighed against the added costs. Often the benefits (including such benefits as improved maintainability) outweigh the costs.

Figure 9.6   The power of re-usable modules (bricks) when building a fence.

Reuse of previous results can be encouraged by having policies and procedures specifying their reuse in specific classes of problems. This reduces expenditure of resources, allowing employees and management to focus energies on areas requiring new solutions.

Indirect Consequences

Management actions often have consequences beyond the immediate project. Those consequences need to be accounted for when assessing leverage. In some cases, indirect consequences can be positive (e.g., strengthening partnerships, improved visibility in new markets, etc.) that increase leverage. But there can also be negative indirect consequences (e.g., damage to relations, depletion of future resources, etc.) that lower leverage. In short, some actions may increase the probability of success of the current project but *decrease* the probability of success of future projects. For example, a product manager might decide to reduce product quality to lower costs and increase near-term profitability. However, this could lead to negative customer experiences and make it more difficult to sell products in the future.

Managers need to consider indirect as well as direct consequences in judging the overall leverage of their actions.

"We'll soon have room for a backyard pool..."

Figure 9.7 Actions can have consequences beyond those intended.

Infrastructure

Lastly, the required resources and time for carrying out specific jobs is dependent on the supporting infrastructure. For example, development of new products will be quicker if a team has a pool of in-house experts to draw upon. Well-equipped research laboratories and rapid prototyping services can also accelerate development. Strong support infrastructure reduce the time and resources needed for executing projects, increasing leverage.

While strong support infrastructures can provide competitive advantages for organizations, managers need to balance the cost of maintaining such infrastructures against longer-term benefits. Infrastructures that build on established strengths (e.g., proprietary technology, broad distribution network, etc.) are especially effective.

"I guess the new fuel mixture isn't right yet..."

"The new fuel mixture is acting almost exactly as predicted by the computer model. A small adjustment will make it perfect."

Figure 9.8 Trial-and-error methods cannot compete with methods leveraging strong support infrastructures.

Summary

In this chapter we described how *leverage*, the net benefit from an expenditure of time and resources, can vary greatly. One of the key jobs of management is maximizing leverage in their organizations.

Managers can do this by keeping their organizations focused, fostering timely communication, synchronizing activities, and minimizing bureaucratic overhead. Building re-useable module libraries and strong support infrastructures can also multiply leverage.

10. Analog World Management

Many people view the management world as a digital world: where choices are either good or bad, projects are successes or failures, decisions are right or wrong. It is human nature to favor simplicity. Black and white choices are easier to comprehend than a continuum of choices.

While it is true that subatomic particles are confined to discrete quantum states, in our macroscopic world human behavior takes on a continuum of values. This means for the purposes of management; it is an analog world - not digital. In an analog world, the effects of actions do not jump in steps as actions are taken, but instead vary smoothly depending on the strength of those actions (see Fig. 10.1 below).

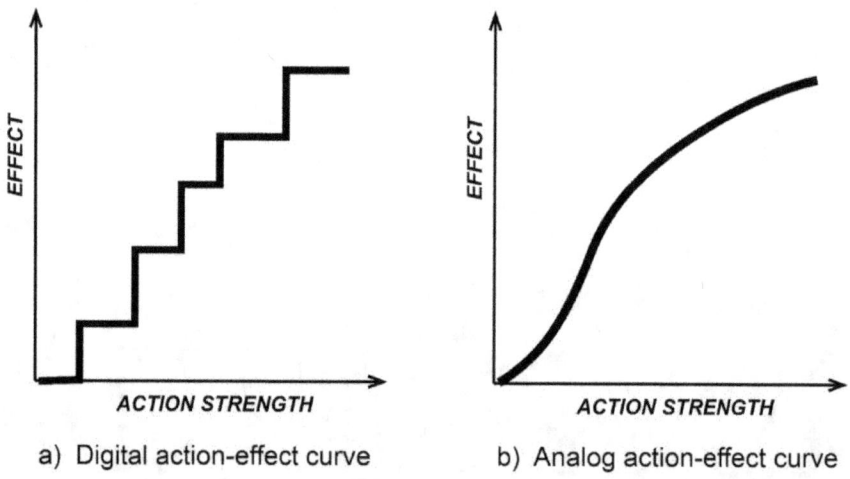

Figure 10.1 Comparison of digital versus analog action-effect curves.

In light of this, there are an infinite range of solutions and actions for any problem, each with its own tradeoffs. For a given business objective, the optimum set of actions depends on the business environment at the conclusion of the project - something that is not knowable at the start. In some cases, the optimum choice may be one that has the flexibility to adapt to a range of situations. The continuum of choices presents opportunities and challenges for managers.

It means managers can "inch" their way towards goals by testing the effects of small actions. Actions resulting in positive results point towards solutions, whereas negative results indicate wrong directions. Incremental approaches provide a systematic way of working towards goals.

In Fig. 10.1(b) a single smooth curve is used to depict analog variation. In the real world, effects will be affected by many action variables – some interacting with each other. In such situations the relationships between variables and effects are represented by multi-dimensional surfaces – something that is difficult to depict graphically on a page. For simplicity, we will continue to represent such relationships as simple two-dimensional curves, with the understanding that each curve represents the effects of many possible actions.

Actions can be large or small depending on their "strength". For example, if newspaper advertising is the action, one measure of its strength would be the size of the ad. Another measure of strength would be the number of times the ad is run.

Incremental Testing

When relationships between actions and effects can be represented by smooth curves, we can predict the effect of larger actions by measuring the effect of small actions (a process called *incremental testing*). Here we are relying on the analog nature of actions and effects and assuming existing behavior will continue when we extend the curve (see Fig. 10.2).

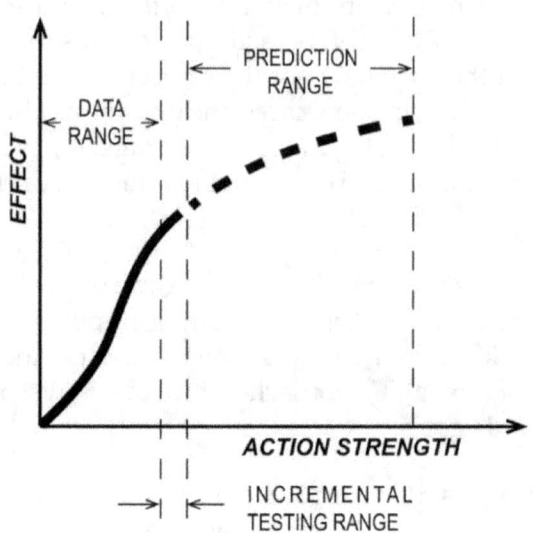

Figure 10.2 Using incremental testing to predict the curve
beyond the data.

Note that the cost of incremental testing is small compared to full
testing, since few resources are required for such tests and the impact
on the system is small (this is especially important if the effects turn
out to be negative).

"I think we should proceed gradually."
"Nonsense, that will take forever..."

Fig. 10.3 Incremental testing can prevent disasters.

Incremental testing is performed iteratively, with predictions interspersed with actual measurements. Management judgment is needed to decide how believable predictions are before performing additional experiments. Subsequent experiments can verify the predictions or generate calibration data that can be used to improve subsequent predictions. Applying this process successively allows us to predict action-effect curves over large ranges. This multi-step process is illustrated below in Fig. 10.4 for two iterations.

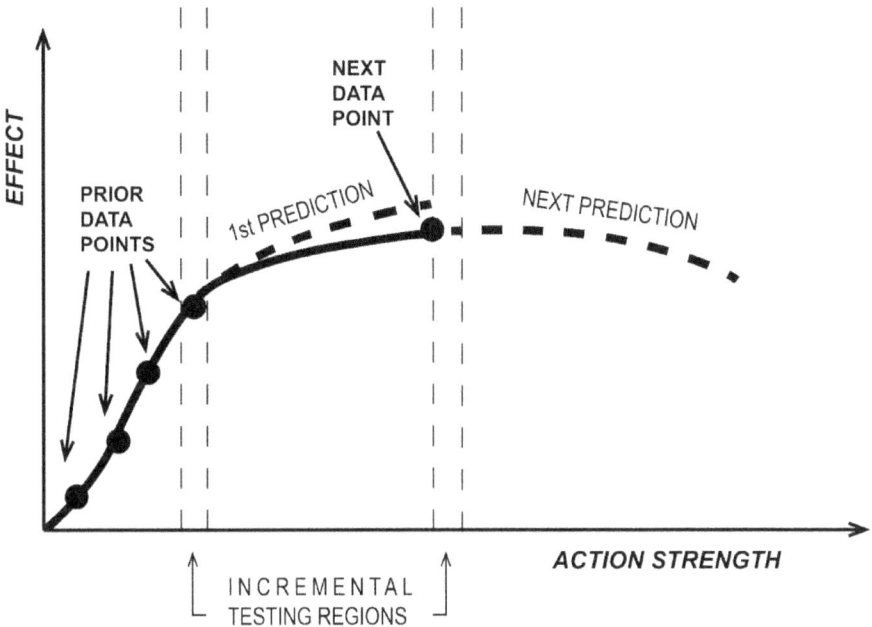

Figure 10.4 Successive incremental measurement-prediction cycles.

In Fig 10.4 trend curves based on existing data and understanding are used to generate the first prediction and define the next actions (next step towards project objectives). After those actions are taken, new measurements ("NEXT DATA POINT" in Fig. 10.4) are compared to the predictions. If they deviate from the prediction, the curves are adjusted to encompass the new data and generate the dashed curve, labeled "NEXT PREDICTION", which is then used for the next predictions. This process is repeated iteratively to progress towards project objectives. This process provides an efficient way of extending knowledge using a limited number of experiments. Note the similarity to the model-prediction techniques previously discussed in Chapter 7.

Let me illustrate this with a practical business problem: determining how much money should be spent on web advertising. Incremental testing can be used to measure the sales increase from small increases in advertising budget. By repeating this process iteratively, the business will be able to map out trend curves to predict the optimum level of such advertising. The optimum is where the cost of more advertising just exceeds the additional benefits. This is shown in Fig. 10.5, which shows the predicted sales curve, as well as the profit curve from those sales. Note the profit curve dips as sales flatten due to the increasing cost of advertising.

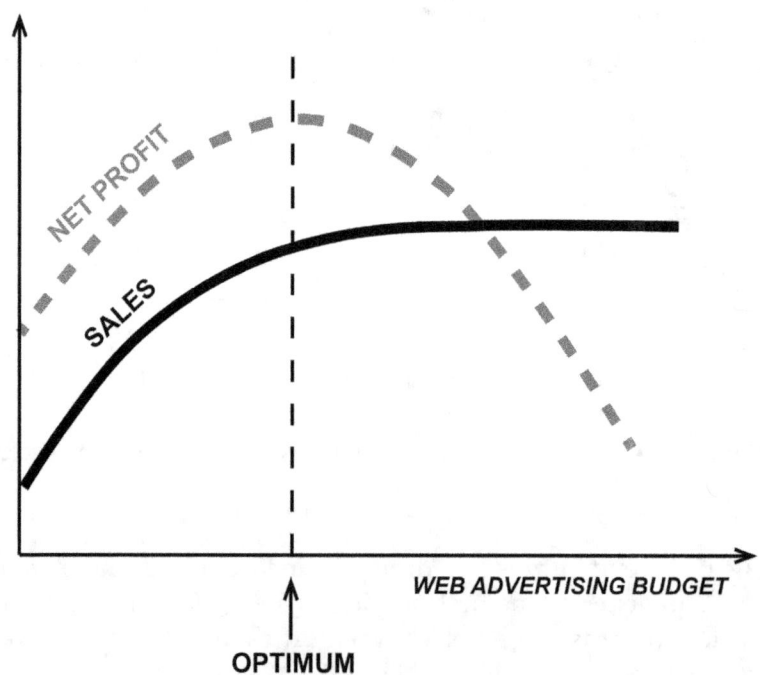

Figure 10.5 Projected sales and profit versus advertising expenditures.

Root-Cause Analysis

Analog action-effect curves also facilitate a process called *root-cause analysis* – an analysis tool for pinpointing the sources of problems. For example, suppose the speed of manufactured widgets varies more than expected, and too many slow widgets are produced. Incremental testing can be used to determine how variations in various manufacturing steps affect widget speed. That information can be combined with the manufacturing control specifications for each step to determine which steps need to be tightened to reduce widget speed variation.

"Wiggling that control
hasn't changed the leak."
(a)

"How about if I wiggle
this control?"
(b)

Figure 10.6   Incremental testing can determine which variables need to be
tightened to improve output.

Model-Based Optimization

One major benefit of being analog is it facilitates automated solution optimization. Recall we said there are many ways of reaching a goal, but not all are equal. Finding the *best* solution is called solution optimization (Fig.10.5 shows one example of solution optimization). Optimization can be easily performed by computers when actions and their effects can be modeled mathematically by smooth curves.

The required action-effect curves can be derived from extrapolations of existing data, incremental testing, and mathematical models of physical effects. For example, in microchip design, physics-based mathematical models can be used to predict circuit behavior as key design variables are changed. Established numerical optimization techniques can be applied to such models to swiftly calculate optimum solutions. Computers can evaluate thousands of variable combinations in minutes using such models, any of which might take months to evaluate using physical experiments. Such *model-based optimization* techniques have revolutionized engineering and development in countless fields.

One might question whether we can believe results from model-based optimization. Most business situations are too complicated to model with theory alone. Real-life business situations are also affected by many variables not included in the models.

Model Calibration

The solution is **model calibration**, a process we discussed previously in Chapter 7, where the models are calibrated to force predictions to fit existing experimental data. This is illustrated in Fig. 10.7.

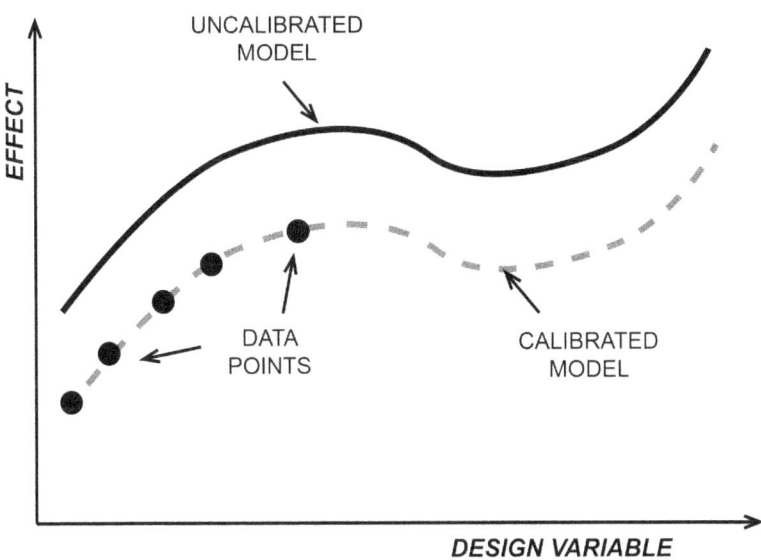

Figure 10.7 Comparison of uncalibrated and calibrated mathematical models.

When models are calibrated, they need only model the *changes* from effects, and not the absolute values.   Such calibrations can compensate for many deficiencies in such models.

For example, suppose the project is to deliver a chip design that is twice as fast as current designs with equal or less power consumption. Chip models calibrated with existing experimental data can be used to predict how chip performance will change as primary design variables are changed. Mathematical optimization techniques applied to those models can automatically determine the best combination of variables that satisfy design goals, namely the lowest power design meeting the 2X speed goal.

Although one cannot guarantee such results will be accurate, they are likely the best that can be done with available data. And as we have said repeatedly, in business the goal is not being 100% correct, but more correct than the competition.

What About Discontinuous Relationships?

Our previous discussions assumed smooth curves can model the relationship between attributes and design variables. In practice, this is only true over limited ranges. Even in an analog world, there are mechanisms that can drastically alter curves when variables exceed certain limits. Although such effects can still be modeled as smooth curves, the curve changes may be so steep that they appear as discontinuous changes.

An example exists in the relationship between speed and voltage in microchip circuits. Normally, increasing the voltage increases the switching speed in circuits. However, if the voltage is increased too much, additional conduction mechanisms occur (e.g., avalanche breakdown, tunneling, etc.) that can cause devices to abruptly malfunction or be destroyed. In this case, the analog design range is for voltages below the onset of such mechanisms.

Markets can also cause the relationships between attributes and variables to be discontinuous. For example, if the peripheral chips supporting a microprocessor are only available in three speeds, microprocessors with speeds other than those that can be supported have no added value. Even though the relationship between a variable and speed may be continuous, the relationship between that variable and value (product price) will be discontinuous (see Fig 10.8) with prices fixed for each supported speed range (depicted by BIN 1, 2 and 3 in Fig 10.8).

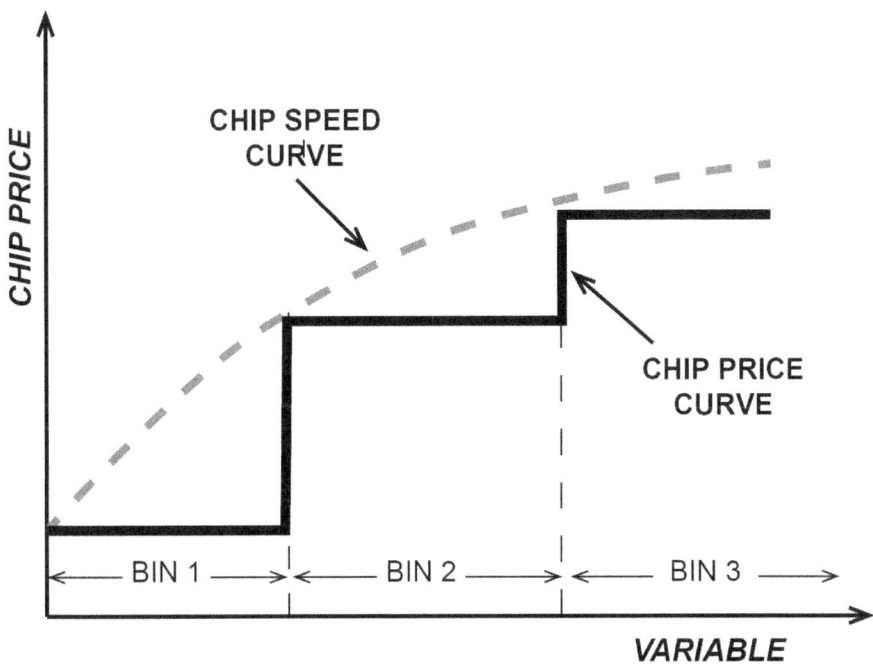

Figure 10.8   Example of how market conditions can introduce discontinuities.

A fuller optimization of this design would require separate design optimizations for each speed range, with potentially different designs and manufacturing for each speed category. Depending on the market size, the added benefits might not warrant the additional design, manufacturing, and inventory costs.

Using Forces to Focus

In the physical world, forces combine and the net force determines how systems change. The analog in the management world is the sum of human activity within a project determines project progress. For purposes of illustration, consider activities separated into two categories: those contributing to project progress and those that do not. I will call the latter "DISTRACTIONS" (they include such activities as personal phone calls, recreational web surfing, social texting, gossiping, etc.).

Obviously, project progress would be greatest if all activities were directed towards project progress. This is not practical in the real world, as there will always be some distractions (from rest breaks, personal matters, miscellaneous chores, etc.), the amount of which will vary. The manager's job is to minimize such distractions and keep them from growing.

If unchecked, a distracted employee may distract other employees, who in turn may distract even more employees. For example, unfounded rumors can spread rapidly, hurting group morale and output. Personal conflicts may cause employees to take sides, spreading conflict and hurting teamwork.

Part of a manager's job is keeping workers focused on project goals. This means providing countering forces to keep distractions to the minimum. In an analog system, the stability point is where forces equal and balance themselves out. This is analogous to a ball in a well (see Fig. 10.9), where the forces moving the ball are cancelled by the walls of the well. Momentary forces can cause the ball to roll up the sides, but it will keep returning to the bottom of the well.

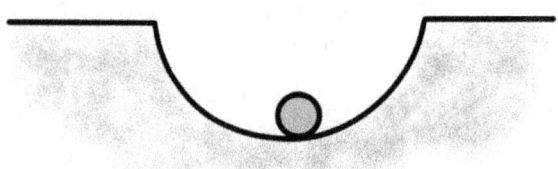

Figure 10.9 The stable point for the ball is the bottom of the well.

Just as for the ball in the well, *managers need to provide counter forces to minimize the effects of distractions.* For example, policies and procedures could be imposed to limit personal phone calls and excessive web surfing during work hours. Formal break periods can reduce fatigue as a distraction. Regularly scheduled employee meetings can be used to communicate business plans and prevent rumors. Concerns about career growth can be mitigated through employee training programs and regular 1-on-1 discussions. More aggressive project schedules can also reduce time for distractions. The goal is to provide forces that prevent distractions from growing.

This requires mangers communicating project goals and their relevance to employee success. For example, if an employee's goal is to gain fame through publications but the company's goal is to develop proprietary technology, the conflict can result in employee dissatisfaction. A compromise solution would be to agree that publications of proprietary technology would be allowed, but only *after* the technology is successfully productized (i.e., in products for sale) and superseded by superior technologies. Another solution would be to seek employees whose primary goal is seeing their ideas realized in successful products.

Figure 10.10 graphically compares a well-managed versus poorly managed work environment.

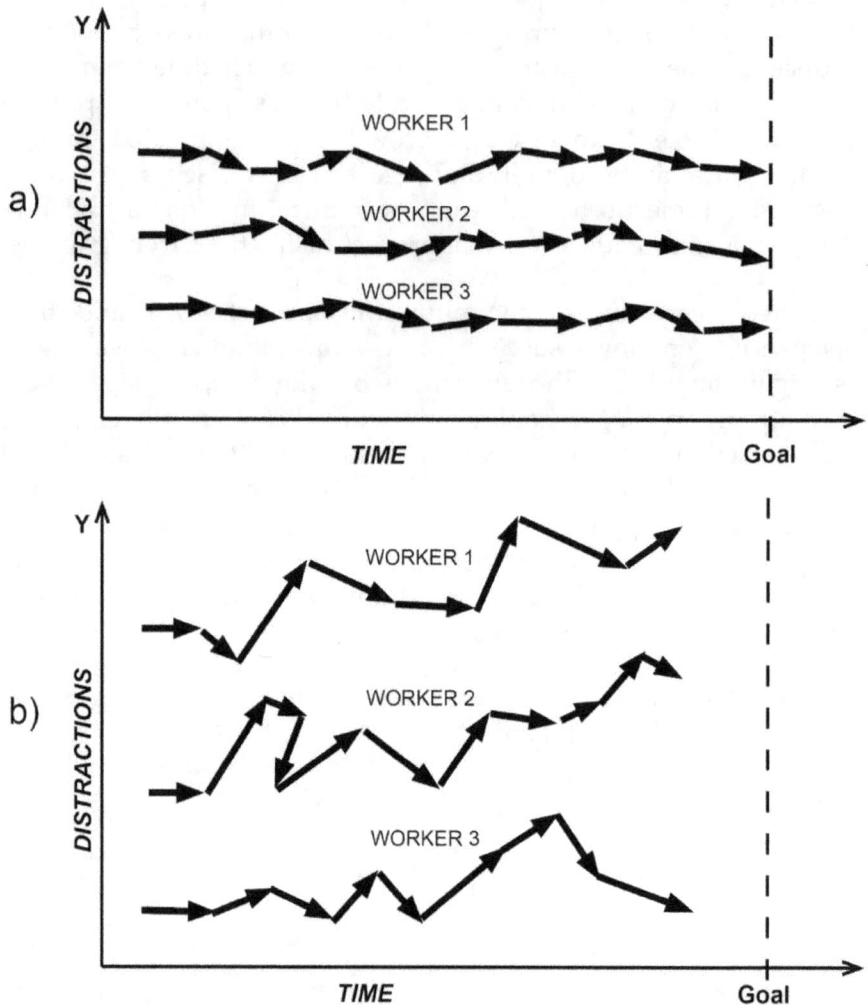

Figure 10.10 (a) Well managed work environment vs. (b) Poorly
managed work environment

Summary

The management world is intrinsically analog in nature – meaning there are a continuum of solutions for any project, each with its own tradeoffs.

The analog nature of the world allows incremental testing and data extrapolation to predict effects beyond existing data by using mathematical models. Such models can be combined with computer-based optimization techniques to find optimum solutions automatically. Such models are also useful for root-cause problem analyses.

In an analog world, systems move towards states where the sum of all forces are balanced. One of the jobs of management is providing compensating forces to minimize distractions and keep employees focused on business goals.

11. Collective Problem Solving

Group problem solving - where teams of people work together to tackle problems - is the norm in business. Its usage varies with company culture, with its use greater in large versus small companies and often more in established versus new companies. In this chapter we will discuss some of the pros and cons of group problem solving.

Benefits of Group Problem Solving

Incorporates More Viewpoints. Each group participant adds his or her knowledge and expertise to the problem-solving process. This expands the pool of information for making decisions beyond that of any individual. Since more information means less uncertainty, groups are better at *selecting lower-risk solutions*. For this to work, each participant must contribute (i.e., voice) his or her opinions and all inputs need to be objectively considered. Participants who remain silent or whose inputs are ignored obviously do not contribute to the process.

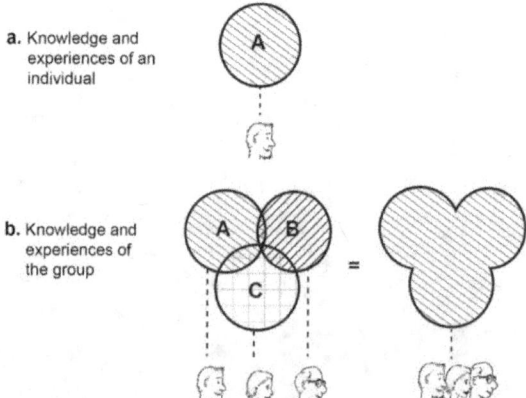

Figure 11.1   The knowledge and expertise of a group is always greater than that of any individual member.

The increase in group knowledge is greatest when the backgrounds of its members are diverse. Common backgrounds (the overlapping areas in Fig. 11.1b) do not expand the knowledge base. Consequently, it is desirable to choose group members with complimentary backgrounds.

Parallel Problem Solving. Groups can develop solutions faster. Not only does each participant contribute different information to the problem-solving process, but each participant adds their brainpower in developing solutions. This can enable groups to make progress more quickly.

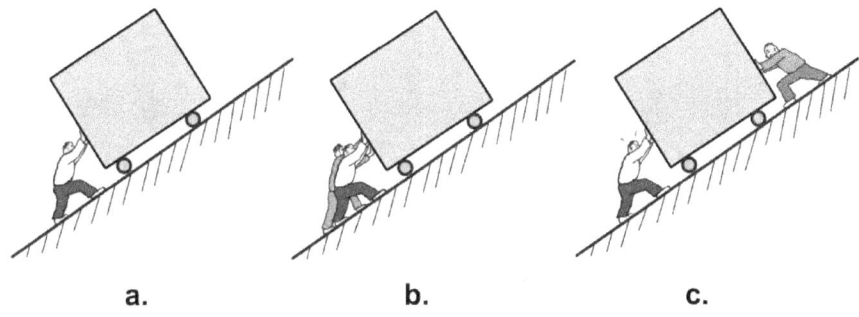

a.   **b.**   **c.**

Figure 11.2 Groups (b) can solve problems faster than individuals (a) since the work can be partitioned among group members. Of course, this is only true if all the members (c) are working towards the same goals.

Promotes Objectivity. Emotions always color personal viewpoints. Individual experiences, prejudices, moods, etc., affect how positive or negative an individual will view specific solutions. Members in a group are unlikely to have the same biases (especially if the group is diverse), so personal emotions will be a lesser factor in group decisions. In general, groups tend to be driven more by objective and logical reasoning. This filtering out of personal biases aids problem solving by reducing irrelevant information in the decision process.

"I think we should forget about supporting existing customers and legacy systems."

Figure 11.3   Groups filter out radical ideas.

Facilitates Buy-In. The best solution is the one that meets project goals with the lowest risk.   However, since every management decision has uncertainties and alternative approaches always exist, not everyone will agree on what that best solution is. Group problem solving can mitigate disagreements as it allows multiple viewpoints to be aired in an open, objective problem-solving process. Group members are more likely to buy into the final decision when they have been part of the decision process.

Downsides of Group Problem Solving

Slower Decision Process. Group decisions usually take more time than decisions made by individuals. For one, extra time is needed to find and assemble group participants. Additional time is also needed to bring participants up to speed and to ensure every member understands project objectives and resources. The solution process also tends to be slower, as more time is needed for communicating and considering the views of each group participant. Not all problems can afford this amount of time, especially if project schedules are very tight. However, when there is sufficient time, group problem solving can result in superior solutions.

Deters Innovation. Group problem solving is centered on consensus decision-making. Consequently, it tends to favor decisions supported by hard data. Therefore radical approaches are less likely to be chosen, as those are the ones with the least amount of supporting data. This is one of the downsides of group problem solving - it not only filters out emotions but can filter out novel ideas. As a result, group problem solving rarely leads to breakthrough solutions or great innovation. Groups are not as good at forecasting the future as talented individuals with vision.

This is a case where management judgment and guidance are crucial. If breakthrough solutions are needed, management needs to define objectives that are aggressive enough to force consideration of innovative solutions. In this case the group's purpose would be identifying the most promising novel solution.

Can Accentuate Political Infighting. Group problem solving sessions can become forums for political grandstanding. More aggressive members may dominate discussions and try to impose their views on the group. Less aggressive members may be wary of voicing their opinions if they feel they will be attacked. Members may also be reluctant to voice positions they think the attending manager would not favor. Such behaviors are contrary to the group problem solving process, which is predicated on open discussions and objective analyses. Management facilitation is key to minimizing political influences in groupthink sessions.

Managers as Facilitators

Group problem solving sessions can benefit from having a senior manager present - one with greater decision-making authority than group participants. In such meetings (commonly referred to as "peers plus one" meetings) the attending manager facilitates group discussions by ensuring inputs from all team members are considered. This includes soliciting inputs from quieter members and limiting the airtime of more vociferous members. The manager can also break deadlocks and limit discussions when decision processes become stalled. The manager can also keep the group focused on project objectives. Lastly, the manager can ensure innovative ideas get adequate consideration by the group.

"Enough, Fred - we understand your position! What are your thoughts, Seymour?"

Figure 11.4 The facilitating manager needs to ensure inputs from all members are considered.

It is also important to remember that the manager of the project (who may or may not be the group facilitator) is still responsible for making final decisions. Group problem solving sessions are primarily used to generate recommendations. Utilization of group problem solving does incur responsibilities, however. If the deciding manager selects a direction different from the group's consensus, the manager needs to explain why.

It is preferable that managers intervene and steer group problem solving sessions away from unacceptable directions to avoid vetoing unacceptable solutions later. Managers need to be careful, however, to not overly control group problem solving sessions – otherwise the open exploration of solutions will be inhibited.

Figure 11.5 Managers need to restrict the solution space to what is acceptable.

Summary

Group problem solving can be a useful management tool for tackling difficult problems. They can lead to superior solutions, faster problem solving, and greater buy-in of final plans.

Goals and objectives need to be clearly defined and understood by all group members for the process to work.

Managers play an important role as facilitators in such sessions: to keep sessions moving in the right direction and to prevent them from becoming political forums.

12. Modularization & Complexity

Adding features to systems becomes increasingly difficult as systems grow in size and complexity. Changes to parts of a system may inadvertently affect other parts of the system, causing unanticipated problems. The likelihood of this happening increases with the size of the system. While comprehensive testing can root out such problems, the number of tests required to accomplish this increases exponentially with system size – making such testing prohibitively expensive when system sizes become very large.

This is a basic characteristic of complex systems, improvements become increasingly difficult as system sizes grow. It is analogous to operating towards the mature end of learning curves. Such problems are especially evident in large software systems, where the probability of introducing "bugs" when new features are added increases greatly with the number of lines of code in the program. Although such problems can be mitigated by keeping systems small, oftentimes the desired functions are not deliverable in small systems.

One solution is to construct the larger system from multiple small systems (called "modules") that communicate with each other in restricted ways. But isn't this just a large system in another guise? The answer is not if we restrict the communication between modules to only what is needed to send and respond to action requests. This is the essence of *modularization,* where large systems are constructed out of smaller interconnected subsystems whose interactions are strictly limited.

This is illustrated in Fig. 12.1 with a system made up of 6 subcomponents. In the nonmodular system (a) each of the six subcomponents can interact directly with each of the other 5 subcomponents, making a total of 15 possible interactions. In the modular system (b) the components are isolated into two groups of three - with only one path for interaction between the groups. This reduces the possible interaction paths to 7, a more than 50% reduction. The potential reductions increase as the number of subcomponents grows.

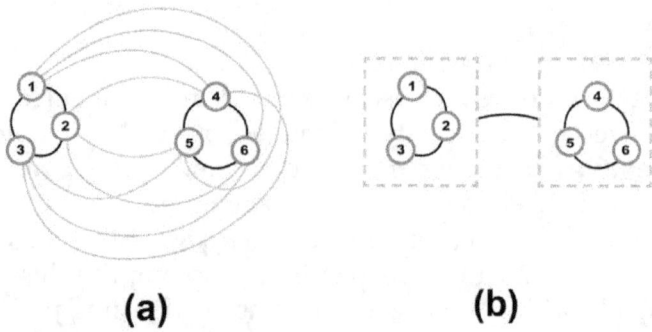

(a)   **(b)**

Figure 12.1 Interactions in non-modular versus modular systems.

This is also how people interact in the real world. Human minds are incapable of comprehending pictures of the world with all its detail. Instead, we focus on less detailed pictures tailored to the task at hand. For example, when we start our car in the morning, we turn on the ignition, look to the rear to ensure there are no obstacles, and back out of the driveway. We assume that turning on the ignition and depressing the gas pedal will cause the car to move. We do not think of how gas is being injected into the engine's cylinders and exploded in a synchronized fashion to generate forces to drive the wheels – that is, unless the car fails to start. In short, we compartmentalize our thinking to focus on the immediate actions we need to take and assume associated actions occur automatically.

There are advantages to having management systems parallel this. Partitioning a large project into many smaller projects or *modules*, each with its own goals and resources, greatly simplifies the management job. Not only are smaller subprojects easier to manage, but it also allows managers to focus resources on the most difficult subprojects (the ones with the greatest risk of failure). It also facilitates parallel development of portions of the project to speed project execution.

To support modularization, project goals need to specify how modules are to communicate in the system. This takes the form of communication protocols specifying the kinds of information each module will exchange with other modules. Provided a module correctly performs the actions requested by the inputs, the module does not need to know the source of the inputs – i.e., does not need to know details of the other modules. This isolation is key to allowing a project to be broken into smaller subprojects or modules.

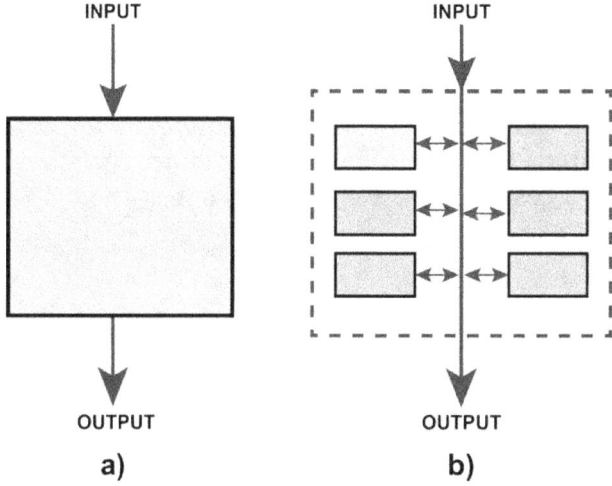

Figure 12.2 Comparison of a non-modular and modular computation system. In (a) the processing is performed by one large processing unit. In (b) processing is split among six processing units, each communicating over a formal communication bus.

Benefits of Modularization

Modularization has significant managerial benefits. Since management modules are smaller managerial jobs with fewer goals and resources – *problems are easier to identify and resolve*. For example, it is easier to detect when module goals are not going to be met than if overall project goals will not be met.

Maintenance is also easier in modular systems. When changes are made to a specific module, it only needs to be tested to ensure it satisfies the interaction protocols specified for it. Provided it does, interactions with other modules will not change and other modules do not need to be retested. This makes it much easier to make changes to a large system.

Furthermore, since module projects are independent of each other, they *can be developed in parallel* in separate project teams, speeding execution of the overall project. Modularization of tasks also facilitates contracting jobs to external vendors, enabling companies to lower labor costs and access capabilities they lack.

Examples of Management Modularization

The automotive industry provides many examples of a modularized management systems. Basic car frames and bodies are typically built in geographically dispersed factories. These frames and bodies are combined with other components (engines, tires, windows, electrical systems, etc.) produced in yet different factories (some owned by external vendors) and assembled as completed automobiles in assembly plants. Each of the components are defined through detailed specifications to ensure they will fit together in the assembled automobile. Component specifications and delivery schedules serve as the interaction protocols in such modular systems. Provided the produced components meet specifications, management of each of the factories is self-contained and localized. Senior management is left to focus on strategic planning and problem areas (e.g., areas not meeting specifications or delivery schedules). In the automobile industry, modularization makes it easy for manufacturers to scale the number of factories. It also allows them to locate factories in the most favorable geographic locations.

Even small management systems can take advantage of modularization. For example, consider a group developing a new database software system. Development tasks could be modularized by having different groups develop user interfaces, data storage, and test suites, with specific module specifications defined for each group. This can speed overall development since all three groups can work in parallel. Active management is still needed, however, to keep modules integrated and to adjust plans when problems arise.

Downsides of Modularization

Modularization does have some negatives, however. For one, it *adds overhead* to a system. Restricting inter-module communication to formal interaction protocols complicates communication, especially for simpler modules. Since all requests are passed to *all* interconnected modules, the communication interface for every module must be capable of interpreting the most complex task any module will ever be called on to perform. This can add significant overhead to modules performing simple tasks - especially modules performing frequent tasks, since this overhead accumulates each time such tasks are performed. For simple tasks, a modularized system will perform more slowly than a non-modularized system.

This problem can be mitigated if the system is architected to keep frequent simple tasks within modules to reduce communication across modules. Since communication within modules is not burdened by restrictive interaction protocols, internal communication can be optimized for speed. In software systems this may require replicating software for simple tasks inside multiple modules. The downside is any future changes to that software will need to be made in every module incorporating that software, increasing maintenance and testing costs.

Another negative in modular management systems is *inflexibility*. Major changes are harder to implement in modular systems. If a module group discovers some of its functions would be easier to implement in a different module group, they cannot simply shift that task to that other group. In modular management systems, task changes require changes to the formal specifications affecting all groups. The bureaucratic overhead of obtaining approvals makes changes expensive. This means it is important that the design of a modular system be optimized at the beginning.

Air traffic control systems are another example of modular systems. Airline pilots fly their prescribed routes without worrying about where other planes are - essentially acting as self-contained modules. Air traffic controllers serve as the communication interface for keeping planes out of each other's way.

Fig. 12.3 illustrates a limitation of modular systems. They can be slow when reacting to unexpected situations.

"Tower, this is AA209, would you please check that heading you gave us again?" "Roger that AA209, just give me a second..."

Figure 12.3 Air traffic controllers as communication interfaces

One last negative: modular systems can *inhibit communication* between employees. By design, each module group operates in isolation to complete their particular tasks. Contact with other groups is limited beyond agreeing on interface specifications (e.g., what and when specific capabilities will be delivered) and reporting progress. This inhibits team building across the organization and can lead to unhealthy inter-group rivalry.

Management Roles in Modularization

The previous examples show management has key roles to play in making modularization work. For one, more planning is required to execute in a modular fashion, as the modules must be predefined along with interaction protocols. The design of modules needs to be optimized around available resources (skills of the staff, available facilities, etc.) and project schedules. For a senior manager, this is equivalent to managing multiple projects simultaneously.

Keeping module projects synchronized is a classic project management job. This requires regularly monitoring the progress of each module. Project tracking tools, such as Gantt charts (an example is shown in Fig. 12.4), are useful for this. In Fig. 12.4 horizontal bars represent each of the tasks in the project, with the length of the bar indicating the time allocated for the task. Tasks are staggered within each group to show each group utilizing only their own resources. This allows each group to pursue their projects separately. The vertical arrows in Fig 12.4 represent dependencies, to indicate when tasks in one group cannot be started until tasks in another group are completed. For example, in Fig. 12.4 Task B3 cannot be started until Task A2 is completed. Likewise, Task C2 cannot be started until Task B2 is completed (e.g., Task C2 might be testing the subsystem put together in Task B2).

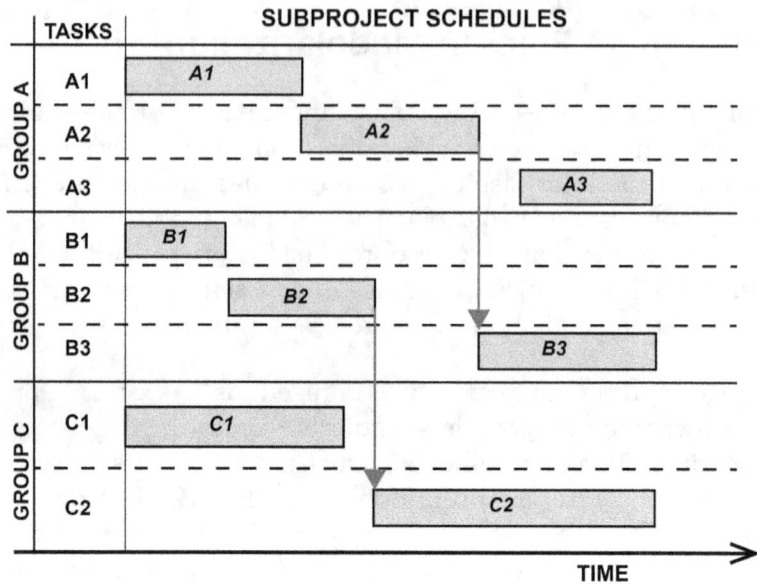

Figure 12.4 Example Gantt Chart.

Such charts are useful for determining the impact on schedules when subprojects take longer than planned. They are also useful for planning the assignment of resources. Those same charts can also be used to determine what plan changes are needed to compensate for subproject delays. Gantt charts can be created using simple spreadsheet programs or generated by commercial Project Management programs.

Multi-Level Abstraction

Our ability to modularize is a unique human strength. It allows us to view large complex systems at multiple levels of abstraction. The most expansive view is one showing the whole system as interconnected high-level functional blocks. The next level are views of details within component blocks. This hierarchical decomposition of a system continues until we reach sub-blocks specifying detailed actions. This hierarchy can be mated to the management hierarchy of an organization, with supervisors managing staff execution in the lower-level modules, and higher-level managers managing the supervisors and monitoring progress and adjusting plans (see Fig. 12.5).

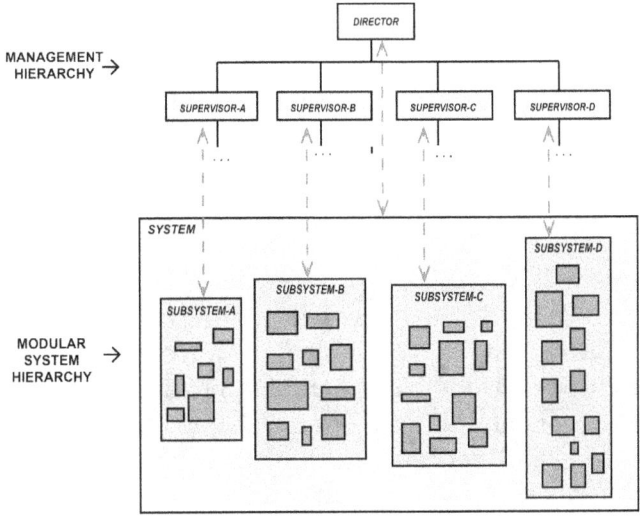

Figure 12.5 Pairing management levels to modular system.

Summary

Modularization, the partitioning of big tasks into smaller independent tasks, is an important management tool. It reduces complexity to manageable levels – allowing large systems to be managed hierarchically. To work, schedules and input/output specifications (goals) for each module need to be rigorously specified. Module progress also needs to be closely monitored to ensure plans are synchronized and remain valid.

Although modularization can affect performance and add overhead, in large systems the benefits outweigh the added cost.

13. Stability & Change

Business Environments Are Inherently Unstable

All businesses are in one of three states: decline, stability, or growth. Those in decline eventually run out of money and fail. Those that are growing are also changing, but in a good way. But what about businesses that are stable with reasonable profits?

Competitors will copy businesses strategies they see are successful. When they copy stable businesses, the added competition will cause profits to fall, causing those businesses to decline. Therefore, even stable businesses need to prepare for change. This is another manifestation of our discussions in Chapter 6: that all learning curves mature and saturate. In short, businesses need to keep changing to stay profitable over the long term.

Since the direction for change is not always clear, changes are best carried out in an incremental trial and error process, to map out the shape of *benefit versus change* curves. Such curves can help managers identify optimum directions for change.

To illustrate this process, consider a hypothetical example. A manufacturer of professional cooking tools, whose profits have been declining, decides to broaden its markets by targeting home cooks. To do this, the company purchases advertising time on cable network cooking shows. The ads attract new customers and sales expand. In response, the manufacturer buys more advertising time and sales increase further. Eventually, increasing advertising fails to expand sales enough to offset the additional advertising costs and company profits begin to fall again. The company then backs off advertising to the level where it was most profitable.

Since the goal is keeping company profits optimized, one might conclude advertising just needs to be maintained at this level. However, changing customer tastes, new competition, technology advances, etc., will alter the optimum point over time. This means the company will need to continually monitor sales and modify strategies when profitability starts to decline.   For example, publishers of traditional paper magazines and newspapers have seen their businesses increasingly supplanted by web-based information services.   Those that have supplemented their offerings with polished on-line versions have been more successful at surviving.

It is the nature of businesses to push the envelope of profitable markets until they are no longer profitable. This lack of stability is an inherent characteristic of competitive business environments.

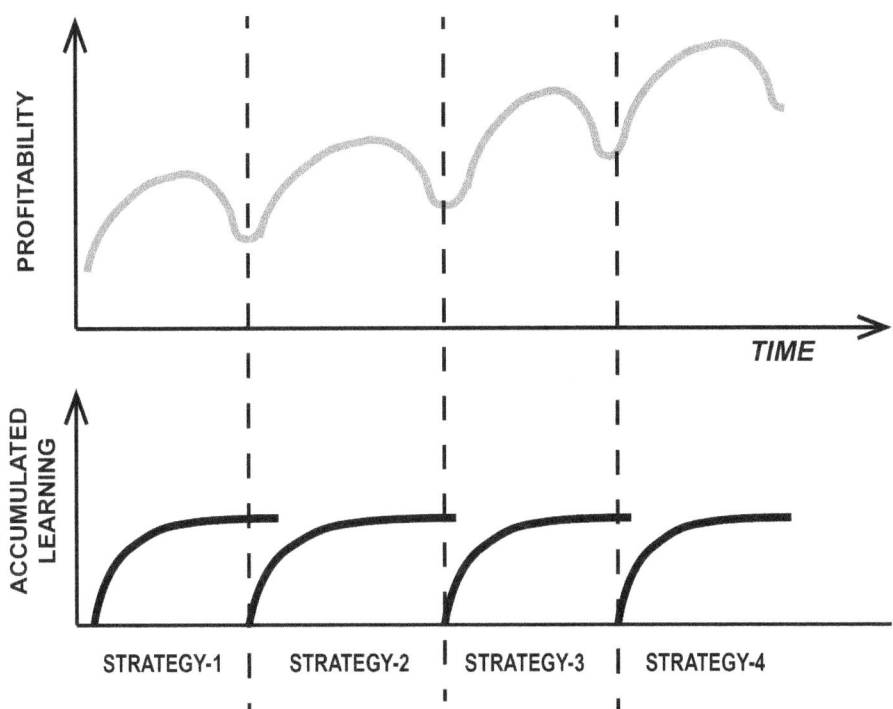

Figure 13.1 Profits are cyclical and correlated with learning curve saturation.

Figure 13.1 depicts the cyclical nature of business and how profitability is aligned with learning curve saturation. For a given strategy, profitability grows as learning grows (e.g., as products improve) then declines when learning saturates. Transitions to new strategies and new learning curves are necessary to maintain profits.

Managing Change

Managers have seemingly contradictory responsibilities – ensuring existing systems are stable and efficient, while also preparing for changes to those systems. The former is needed to provide workers with stable work environments. On the other hand, change is necessary to stay competitive in a dynamic world.

Fortunately, managers need not be schizophrenic to handle these contradictory responsibilities - they simply need to view them as time-differentiated tasks.

Workers require stability most during the period of their project assignment. Stability allows them to plan and focus. Consequently, efforts should be made to keep work environments stable for the duration of a project. Barring emergencies, changes during a project should be avoided. In short, *the time scale for stability is project duration.*

Changes to the work environment after a project is completed is less of a problem. Plans for *new projects* can include additional resources and activities to facilitate any changes. Thus, *changes are least disruptive when made between projects.*

Large organizations often have many simultaneous projects, each beginning and ending at different times. For such organizations there will never be a single time for change that is optimum for all parts of an organization. A simple solution is to delay change in parts of the organization that are in the midst of projects - in other words, *change is best implemented in a phased manner* across such organizations.

"Stop the work! The owner now wants a basement!"

Figure 13.2   Plan changes during a project can be disruptive.

Why Change Can Be Difficult

The challenge for management is how to institute change without disrupting current operations.   Change does not come easily in established organizations, which tend to settle into comfortable operating modes. Recall our discussion of analog systems in Chapter 10, and the analogy of a marble sitting in a depression in Fig 10.9 (reproduced below in Fig. 13.3).

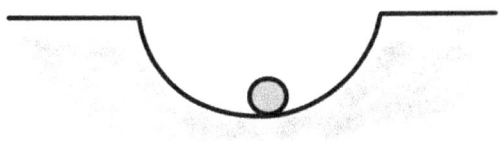

Figure 13.3   Resistance to change depicted by a marble in a depression.

Organizations tend to settle into states where external forces are balanced.   This is especially true in established organizations operating near mature ends of learning curves. Employees in such organizations tend to be comfortable, since they know what to do and have track records for doing it well. These are "comfort zones" for an organization. Unfortunately, this can cause organizations to become complacent and resistant to change. Organizational momentum favors continuing in the same direction. In such situations, management-initiated forces are needed to bring about change.

For example, consider a hypothetical company whose main product is a profitable line of high-performance notebook computers. Management senses the computer market is moving towards tablet computers and has decided to enter those markets but wants to keep its leadership position in notebooks. If management simply makes across the board cuts in the notebook division to free up resources for tablet development, they will be communicating the following to notebook employees:

1. The company is no longer committed to notebooks.

2. Reducing costs in notebooks is a priority.

Each of these messages is a "management force" that affects employee behavior. For example, they may cause notebook divisions to seek cheaper, lower quality components for its notebooks. The reductions in notebook staffing may also degrade customer support, quality control, and development of new notebooks. The result would be less competitive notebook products. This could leave the company vulnerable if it was relying on continued income from leadership notebooks to support its move into tablet computers.

A better approach would be *targeted* reductions in the notebook division, phasing out the least profitable products (i.e., the ones at the mature end of their learning curves) and strengthening the most profitable notebook products - the ones that are most competitive and generate the most profits.

Doing so would instead communicate the following management messages to employees:

1. Unprofitable products have no future in the company.

2. Competitive products that are profitable will continue to be supported.

3. The company is open to exploring new areas of profitability.

These messages are management forces that tell employees what is required for success inside the organization. For example, they encourage employees working on weak products to seek new opportunities (e.g., by transferring to other programs). It also says new product designs (tablet or otherwise) cannot be "me-too" products, but need to be competitive and profitable.

Since the desire to succeed is a driving force for all employees, these changes modify the balance of forces within the work environment. Prior to making these changes, familiarity and comfort was the stable state for employees. After the changes, the stable state adds expectations for change and continued improvement. The new state better aligns employee motivations to the organization's goals. This is illustrated in Fig. 13.4 below, where the management forces are shown as arrows.

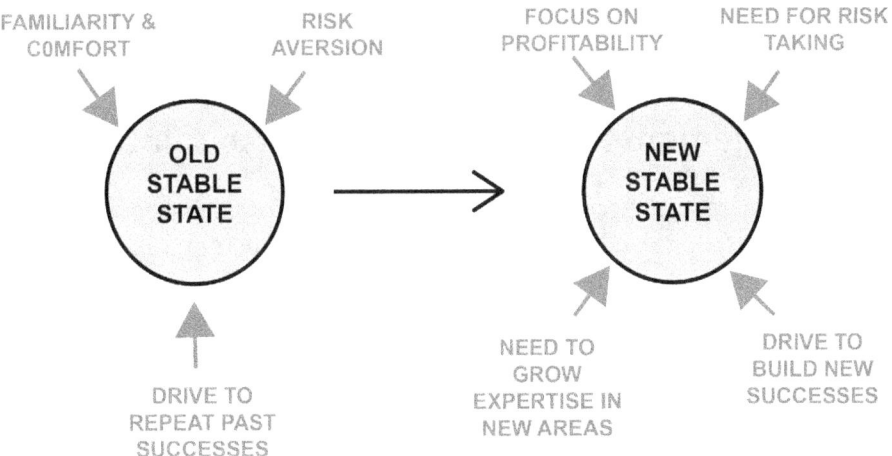

Figure 13.4 Diagram illustrating how management forces can change the stable state.

Old stable state　　　　　　New stable state

Figure 13.5 Corresponding people picture to Fig 13.4

The old stable state represents the status quo comfort zone. For employees, it means following paths based on past successes that offer little challenge. Management forces can change the stable state to the one shown on the right. This is a less comfortable state for employees, but one better aligned to the organization's needs.

Management Forces versus Resource Allocation

Changes to resources (e.g., changing headcount in an area) can clearly also be used to bring about change. Such changes are best viewed as a management force tactic. For example, decreasing headcount in an area will show management wishes to deprioritize activity there.

Management Force Techniques

Management forces for change are most effective when they are targeted. Some methods for targeting management change forces are given below:

1. Leverage long-term objectives and strategies

Use industry trend data and visions to define long-range roadmaps for the organization. Require new projects to be consistent with goals in the roadmaps. Doing so will gradually align future projects with the roadmap.

2. Leverage employee goals

Employees have personal goals and aspirations which can be leveraged to bring about organizational change. Employees whose personal ambitions will be furthered by planned changes in an organization can be recruited as champions for those changes. Active support by employees adds credibility to change plans. This, of course, requires management to be aware of the goals and aspirations of its employees. As we mentioned previously, regular 1-on-1 meetings between supervisors and their employees can help here.

3. Communicate change plans

Future changes are not a priority for most employees, who are primarily focused on their immediate assignments. As a result, planned changes need to be broadly communicated to ensure employees know they are coming. Such changes are best communicated in groups versus 1-on-1 meetings. Not only is this managerially more efficient, but it ensures everyone gets the same message at the same time – reducing misunderstanding.

4. Tailor the change strength to the desired rate of change

If the needed changes are to occur gradually over a long period of time, management forces can be kept small to minimize disruption to current operations. For example, if the change is to improve overall quality, it could be implemented by gradually increasing quality goals (as specified in metrics) for new projects. Disruptions can also be minimized if the changes are first prototyped and debugged in isolated organizations.

Conversely, if changes need to occur rapidly - for example, to respond to sudden market shifts or emergencies - managerial forces need to be strong. Projects have a momentum that favors continuing in the same direction. It takes strong managerial leadership to alter existing directions. Examples of strong managerial change forces include canceling projects, personnel reorganizations, and formation of task forces.

5. Ensure management forces are consistent

Multiple management forces combine. Forces in the same direction produce a stronger net force. Conversely, management forces in contrary directions can cancel each other resulting in a weaker overall force.

If change is a priority, minimize counter forces - at least temporarily. For example, formal policies and procedures for keeping an organization stable are managerial forces that deter change. It may be appropriate to temporarily suspend some procedures if rapid change is needed. This is illustrated in Fig 13.6, where the balance of forces has been changed by reducing the emphasis on maintenance and documentation and increasing the emphasis on development.

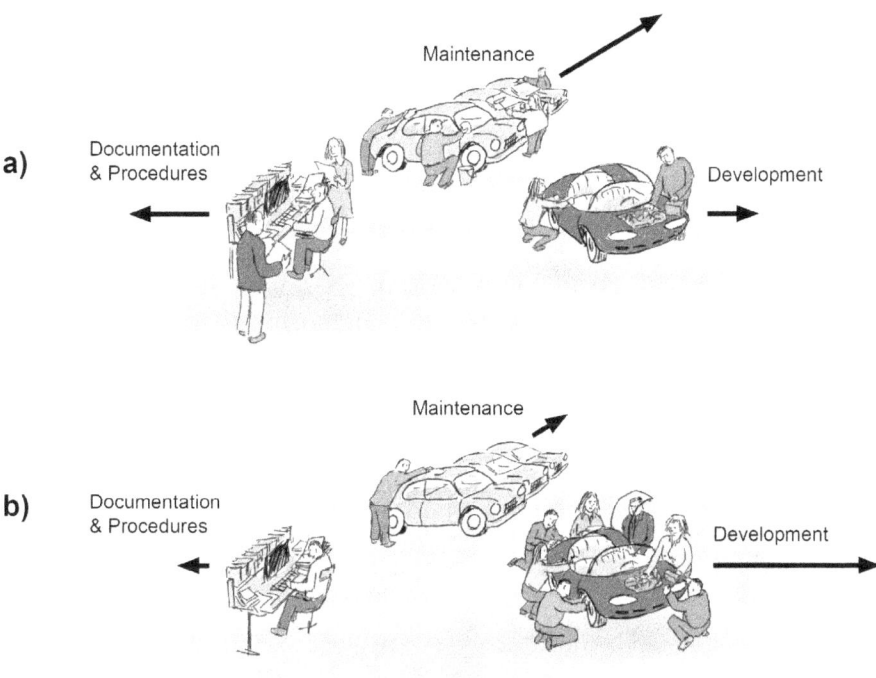

Figure 13.6   Management forces are changed from a) to b) to strengthen
development. The length of the arrows denotes management emphasis
(i.e., force) on documentation, maintenance and development.

Short versus Long-Term Forces

At this point it is worthwhile saying a few words about short versus
long-term forces.

Short-term forces are forces applied for a short duration. They are
often used to adjust projects that are deviating from plan. For
example, if a project team member is falling behind schedule, short-
term managerial forces might include warnings by the employee's
supervisor or a temporary increase in resources.

Conversely, long-term forces are applied continually. Example long-
term forces include enhanced metrics goals to promote continued
improvements in quality and efficiency. Such forces alter the overall
work environment and culture.

Summary

Business environments are inherently dynamic, with changes inevitable. Managers have contradictory roles: maintaining stable work environments for employees while also initiating change to address future challenges.

Ideally, work environments should be stable during a project's duration, and major organizational changes implemented between projects. In both cases managerial forces play key roles - both for maintaining stability and bringing about needed change.

Managers need to be aware of all the forces affecting employee performance - including personal forces. To maximize productivity, those forces need to be targeted to ensure employee motivations are aligned with the goals of the organization.

14. Core Competencies & Planning

The leading companies are stronger than their competitors. Their strengths might be in technology, innovation, manufacturing, service, quality, sales, marketing, or distribution. Those strengths can be local or global. For example, one company's strength might be from having franchises at superior locations versus their competition. Another company's leadership might stem from its global network of sales and support outlets. Still another company's strength might be its superior technology. The areas of competitive advantage are the *core competencies* of the company. These are the areas where the company is stronger than its competitors. Managers need to be aware of their core competencies.

And why is it so important to be a leader in business? Why isn't being good enough sufficient? There are many businesses that are not leaders but profitable, especially in underserved areas with few competitors. For example, opening a grocery store near a new subdivision can be quite profitable if there are a scarcity of supermarkets. There are also marginal businesses whose low profit margins attract few competitors (e.g., door to door selling of cosmetic products).

The challenge is remaining profitable over the long term. Business is inherently a competitive endeavor. If one discovers a good way to make money, others will copy that approach, increasing competition and reducing growth and profits. Customers seek value. They may shop at the second best and third best vendor – but their repeat business will gravitate towards vendors providing the most value for their money. If a business is not one of the leaders, competition will cause it to eventually become unprofitable.

Core Competencies Drive Business Planning

That is why business planning requires knowing your competition and where your products or services add value. This understanding is key to developing good business plans. The areas of competitive advantage determine the size of a company's market. For example, if the core competency of a car dealership is being the only authorized BMW auto dealer in a specific region of a city, then its target market are BMW buyers in that area. Unless that dealership possesses other advantages (other core competencies: such as superior service, greater selection, more attractive showrooms, etc.), its target market would not be all BMW buyers in the city. Entrepreneurs sometimes confuse the size of the total market (e.g., all BMW buyers in this example) as being their target market. Doing so can overestimate growth projections, dilute marketing efforts, and lead to unrealistic business plans.

Conversely, if one's core competencies (areas of competitive advantage) are too specialized, the target market may be too small to profitably support the proposed business.

The Role of Business Planning

How does a company determine if its core competencies are sufficient? A good tool for doing this is the formal business planning process alluded to in Chapter 5. As previously discussed, its basic form consists of the five steps shown in Fig. 14.1:

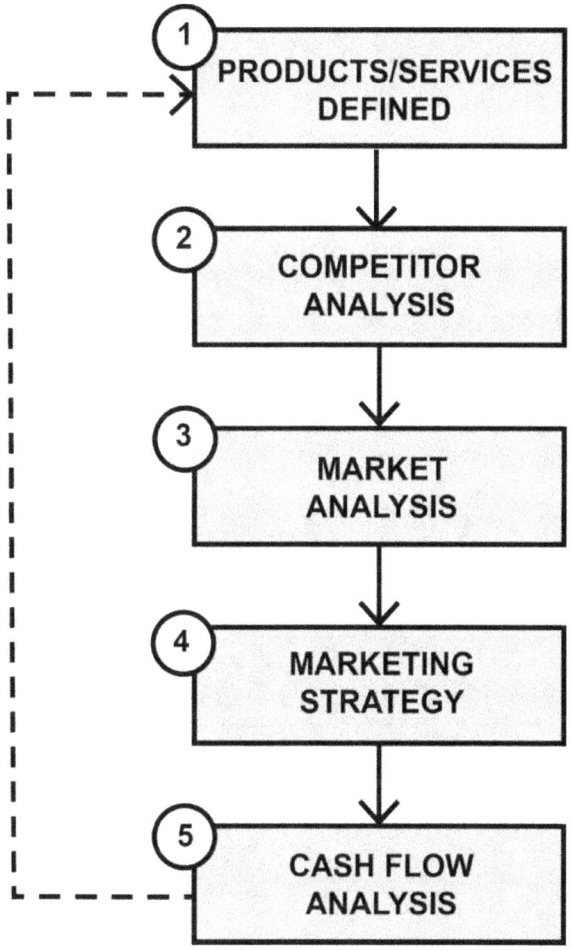

Figure 14.1 Basic Business Plan

1. **Definition of Business Product or Services:** Clear description of planned business offerings and customers.

2. **Competitor Analysis**: Comparison to similar offerings by competitors. This includes comparisons to alternative ways of filling the same customer needs.

3. **Market Analysis**: Identification of customers that would be attracted to planned offerings given the competition. These are the target customers for the business.

4. **Marketing Strategy**: How target customers learn of the offerings from this business.

5. **Cash Flow Analysis**: This is a month-by-month estimation of revenue (money coming in) minus expenditures (money going out) to project the cash flow. This can be done using a simple spreadsheet – an example of which is shown in Fig 14.2. Income in the cash flow analysis depends on the pricing of products and services, plus the projected growth of customers over time. The latter will depend on the Market Analysis and Marketing Strategy (#3 and #4 above). Cash flows in new businesses are typically negative initially, as it takes time to grow customers. The cash balance is also calculated to show the total money remaining in the company each month.

EXAMPLE CASH FLOW ANALYSIS

	JAN 2020	FEB 2020	MAR 2020	APR 2020	MAY 2020	MAY 2020	...
PRODUCT SALES	0	0	50,000	100,000	150,000	160,000	...
SERVICES INCOME	0	0	1,000	1,000	1,500	2,000	...
INVESTOR MONEY	300,000	0	0	0	0	0	...
CASH IN-FLOW	300,000	0	51,000	101,000	151,500	162,000	...
PRODUCT MFG COST	25,000	0	0	0	10,000	0	...
FACILITY LEASE	2,000	2,000	2,000	2,000	2,000	2,000	...
REMODELING EXPENDITURES	10,000	0	0	0	0	0	...
EQUIPMENT EXPENDITURES	15,000	0	0	0	0	0	...
INSURANCE	200	200	200	200	200	200	...
SALARIES	60,000	60,000	125,000	125,000	125,000	125,000	...
MARKETING EXPENDITURES	500	500	500	500	500	500	...
DELIVERY & TRANSPORTATION		100	100	100	200	250	...
UTILITIES EXPENDITURES	100	100	200	200	200	200	...
MAINTENANCE	0	50	50	50	50	50	...
CASH OUT-FLOW	112,800	62,950	128,050	128,050	138,150	128,200	...
NET CASH FLOW	**187,200**	**-62,950**	**-77,050**	**-27,050**	**13,350**	**33,800**	...
CASH BALANCE	**187,200**	**124,250**	**47,200**	**20,150**	**33,500**	**67,300**	...

Figure 14.2 Example spreadsheet showing initial months of cash flow (all numbers in $).

These five steps are normally performed sequentially. Steps #2 and #3 require market research to understand the competitive advantages of the proposed business offerings, which in turn drives Step #4. Step #5 integrates the analyses from the first four steps by adding estimations of expenses (facility lease rates, insurance premiums, materials costs, labor costs, advertising costs, ...) plus proposed pricing of products/services and assumed sales growth to generate an estimate of cash flow for the business.

This cash flow analysis needs to be carried out for enough months to predict two points: (i) the *break-even point*, when cash flows are no longer negative, and (ii) when cash flows (or income) reach the *target goals* for the business.

Provided the analyses in the business plan is performed objectively, the projected cash flow in Step #5 is a "best guess" of income from the business. If the analysis shows the business runs out of cash before the break-even point (i.e., cash balance becomes negative), or the business takes too long to reach target goals, the plan needs to be changed. Changes might include injecting additional investor money to push out the break-even point, more aggressive marketing to accelerate customer growth, or higher product pricing to improve profitability. The dotted return line in Fig 14.1 shows this is an iterative process. If the predicted cash flow in a plan is unacceptable, Steps #1 is modified and Steps #2 through #5 repeated until an acceptable plan is found. This process ensures that, on paper at least, there is a plan that meets business goals. This process is useful for screening out plans that are unlikely to succeed. It is also useful for understanding which core competencies are most important.

The cash flow projections in Step #5 (Cash Flow Analysis) is essentially a "score" of the business plan. Some might question the accuracy and value of such projections, since they are based on assumptions that cannot be accurately known during the planning phase. Provided those assumptions utilize the best available data, such projections still provide an objective "scoring" of the business plan.

The same kind of planning applies equally to nonprofit companies. The only difference is the primary source of income for those companies will be grants and donations from organizations and individuals subscribing to the company's mission. Thus, the paying "customers" are granting organizations, not end-users of the company's services.

Business plans allow many different business strategies to be "tested" on paper. Since "paper tests" are always cheaper and faster than real-life testing, it allows more plans to be evaluated and helps managers find a good plan.

For example, suppose a company is thinking of increasing market share by expanding color options in its product line. Increased product choices may please customers, but might not expand market share if most of those customers would have purchased existing products without the added colors. Business planning is a useful tool for examining the tradeoffs. Competitor and Market Analysis (Steps #2 and #3 in Fig. 14.1) can be used to estimate the increase in market share from adding more colors. The added cost of manufacturing, inventory, and marketing of the extra product colors can then be included in Step #5 to compare final cash flows of "more colors" versus "no more colors" plans to show whether such a change will lead to increased profits.

Importance of Enhancing Core Competencies

Aggressive companies monitor the strengths and weaknesses of competitors to find areas where they can develop competitive advantages. Competitores with static core competencies are good targets, since almost all capabilities can be improved on.

This is illustrated in Fig. 14.3, which shows the "LEADER" company that pioneered the entry into a new market at time **t1** is further down the learning curve than later entrants in that market at times **t2** and **t3** ("FOLLOWER-1" and "FOLLOWER-2"). Notice later entrants do not start at the very beginning of the curves, since they can learn from what the leader has already done. Provided the LEADER continues down its learning curve it will maintain its learning advantage over competitors.

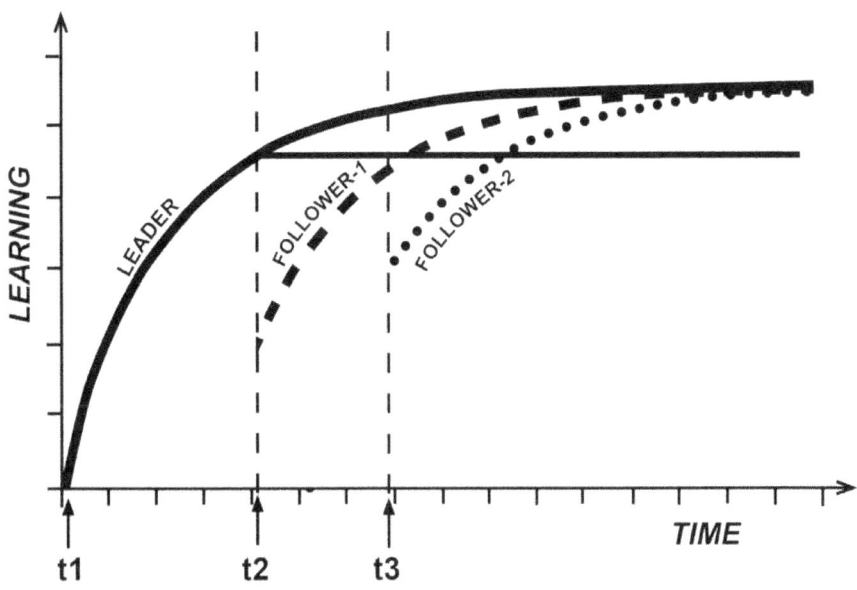

Figure 14.3 Leader and follower learning curves

However, if the Leader were to stop learning (i.e., improving), say at time t2, and follow the solid horizontal line shown in Fig. 14.3, later entrants (the Followers) will eventually surpass it in learning. This means pioneering companies need to continually develop their strengths (continue learning) to stay the leader.

In other words, core competencies need to be continually enhanced if they are to remain core competencies.

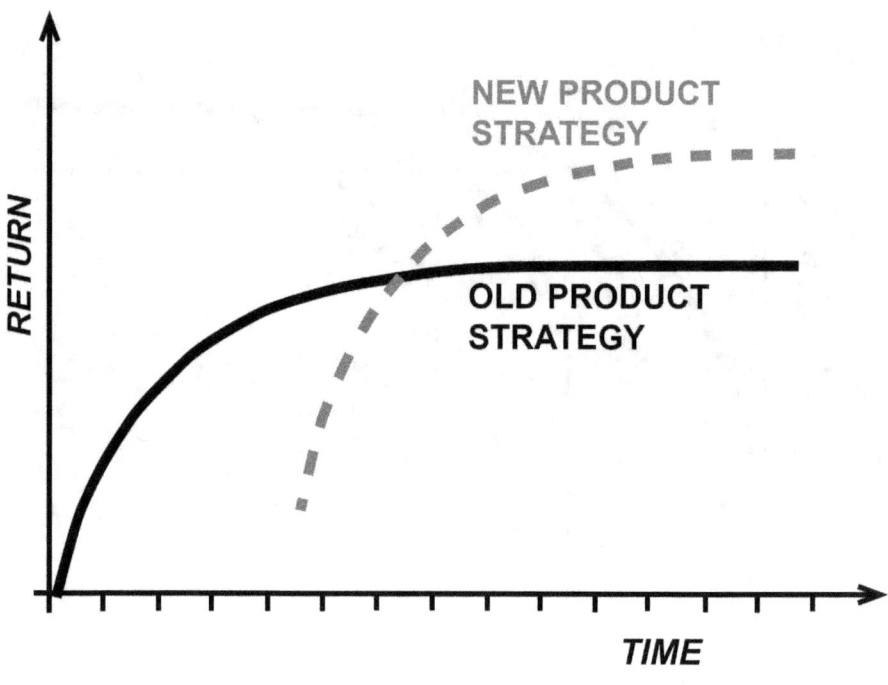

Figure 14.4   Crossing of new and old learning curves

Leveraging Core Competencies for New Areas

As we discussed in Chapter 6, market leaders are also vulnerable to new approaches. Although profits with new approaches may start lower, if they later surpass existing learning curves they can take over market leadership (see Fig. 14.4). Building core competencies is more than refining existing processes; it also includes exploring new approaches to build core competencies for the future.

This is an area where the market leader possesses some advantages, since they should have a better understanding of customer needs. New approaches that address the shortcomings of existing approaches are obvious areas for exploration.

However, the market leader can still miss entirely new product classes – ones that customers were unaware they needed. Such products can supplant existing product classes. For example, advances in mobile devices have led to smartphones replacing conventional cameras for most people.

"We know you love our smartphones, but we wonder if you want any changes... maybe more colors?"

Figure 14.5   Getting customer feedback is useful, but not always sufficient.

Market leaders need to avoid being overly-wedded to existing product strategies. If they stay with old strategies until competitors with different approaches impact their business, they will become followers instead of leaders.

Summary

Successful companies know their core competencies – areas where they have advantages over their competition. Business plans need to be based on a realistic understanding of those competencies.

Key competencies need to be continually enhanced or replaced if a company is to stay competitive. Knowledge about the limitations of current products and services can be used to drive development of superior approaches before competitors.

15. Thinking Ahead

The most successful managers think ahead. While there are management jobs whose focus is more short-term (e.g., production line supervision, quality control monitoring, etc.), such jobs can still benefit from long range thinking.

There are two reasons why thinking ahead is important even for managers focused on short-term tasks. For one, longer range changes in a company or business environment often result in changes in short-term jobs. Being aware of such trends helps managers prepare for such changes. Second, any advantages from superior short-term practices will diminish over time, since competitors will copy those practices.

This can be seen in the context of learning curves in Fig 15.1. **A** is the market leader, and a pioneer on its learning curve. However, if it maintains the same practices (i.e., stays on the same learning curve), competitors copying its practices (**B** and **C**) will eventually reach the same level and eliminate **A**'s advantage, since all learning curves saturate over time.

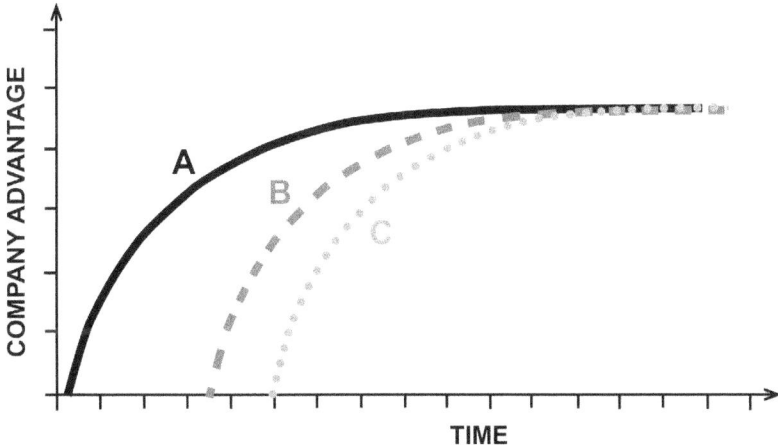

Figure 15.1 Three companies starting the same learning curve at different times.

A real-life example of this is the development of netbooks, the low-priced, limited-feature, notebook computers introduced around 2007. Their light weight and low cost made them popular initially, and initially they sold well and enabled companies like ASUS and Hewlett Packard to capture market share from traditional personal computer companies. But soon nearly every computer company introduced their own version of a netbook, splitting the market among many vendors. Unfortunately, the size of the netbook market turned out to be small. Many customers found them underpowered and their screens too small, relegating them as specialized travel computers. The introduction of tablet computers in 2011 and larger screen smartphones were the final nails in the netbook coffin - as customers favored them as travel computers. The result was plummeting sales of netbooks and shrinking profits for all.

For management, the challenge is allocating the right amount of resource for future contingencies. Allocating too much robs resources from current programs. Focusing only on the near-term, however, leaves organizations vulnerable to future change. Ideally, resources should be balanced between near and long-term risks to minimize overall risk. This requires an assessment of what changes are likely in the future.

Identifying Market Changing Trends

Thinking ahead requires identifying trends that are expected to change the market. *Trends can be local*, such as gentrification of a neighborhood, where the customer base is increasingly affluent and the demand for high quality goods grows. Opening a bargain-basement store in such a neighborhood is probably unwise.

Trends can also be global. Technology advances are the most common cause of global change. However, technological advances can affect many areas, and their effect on markets is not always obvious.

Consider the example of operating systems (the software managing the internal operations inside a computer) for personal computers. Such software is routinely enhanced to support new PC features (e.g., better graphics, faster communication, improved ease-of-use, etc.). The downside is such enhancements also increase the complexity of the software, which can degrade computer performance unless there are commensurate improvements in computing hardware (i.e., faster PC's). For customers not needing the enhanced features, the benefits from such operating systems changes are negative. Their PC's will be slower unless they also upgrade to faster hardware. Such customers resent having to upgrade their computers just to maintain previous levels of functionality. This is another case of learning curve saturation, where gains become increasingly small and costly.

The greatest hazard of not looking ahead is missing paradigm shifts. Microchip advances have allowed portable, battery-powered computers to meet a growing proportion of people's computing needs (web browsing, email, word processing, etc.). This has led to mobile tablets and smartphones replacing many PC's.

This is illustrated in Fig. 15.2 below, which compares two different computing approaches: **A**, which emphasizes performance, and **B**, which emphasizes low power consumption. At the earlier time T1 (the dotted curves in Fig. 15.2), approach **B** was unable to deliver enough performance for basic computing needs, so **A** was the only choice for general computing - relegating approach **B** to specialized, low-power applications. However, at a later time T2 (the solid curves in Fig. 15.2), microchip advances have enabled *both* **A** and **B** to meet basic computing performance needs. The difference is **B** meets them at a lower power consumption point than **A** (**Pb** vs. **Pa**), making it the better choice for mobile computing, relegating approach **A** to specialized, high-performance computing applications.

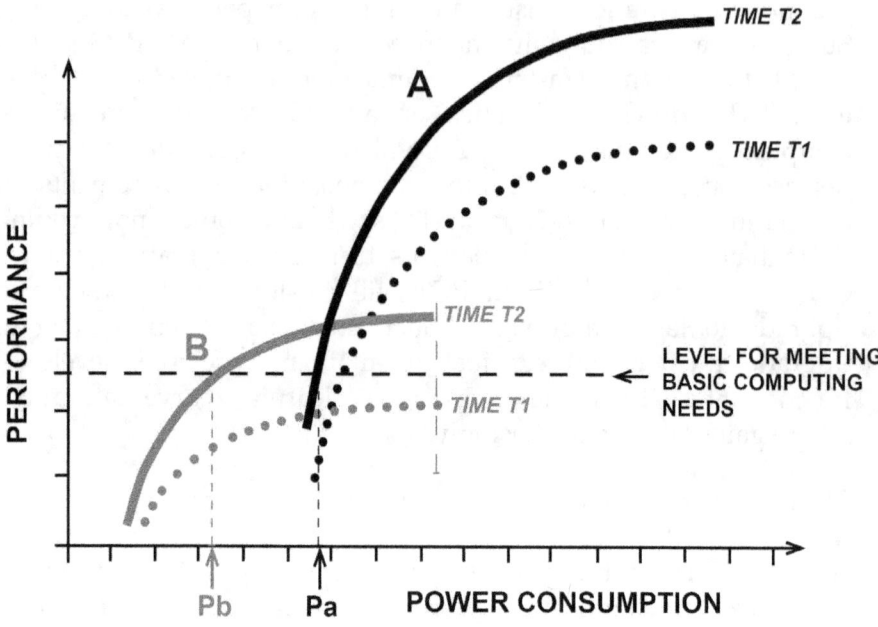

Figure 15.2 Comparison of two different computing approaches.

The takeaway is the optimum business strategy changes over time due to changes in technology, market demand, and competition.

Unanticipated events also alter markets and strategies. For example, the global Covid-19 Coronavirus Pandemic has affected markets dramatically by greatly reducing travel and increasing the number of people working at home. This has led to an upsurge in demand for personal computers to support work at home, remote video conferencing, and on-line learning. Tablet computer sales have also increased. In contrast, the demand for more powerful mobile smartphones has weakened somewhat due to the reduced travel. The message is unforeseen events can alter previous trends.

Predicting change is one of the more difficult challenges for management. Struggling on the tail end of an old learning curve when the rest of the industry is heading down a new superior learning curve is to be avoided. Diligent monitoring of trends and their effect on strategies is key.

For example, the microchip advances that made ultraportable computers possible were predictable. As we mentioned previously (in Chapter 6), for more than 50 years microchip advances have followed a cost-reduction learning curve described by **Moore's Law**, in which chip performance/price approximately doubled every 18 months.

Another global trend is the **shrinking cost of manufacturing**. Global manufacturing and automation have significantly lowered the cost of manufacturing. For some sophisticated products (like smartphones) the manufacturing cost is less than 5% of the product cost. Advances in automation promise to continue this trend, with manufacturing a shrinking proportion of the costs versus components, design, and marketing. The shrinking of manufacturing costs is expected to extend to low-volume products with the growth of 3D-printing technologies. This means a product whose advantage is its ease of manufacture will be less of an advantage in the future. Conversely, product designs that optimize the use of lower cost materials and components will be a growing advantage.

Component, such as screens, batteries, and microchips, are items that can usually be purchased from many vendors. Volume leaders will have an advantage here, as they can negotiate lower prices for such components because of their larger purchase quantities.

This leaves the remaining differentiators: **design, marketing, and service**. Better-designed products work better, are more attractive, and easier to sell. Strong marketing programs can help publicize and communicate product advantages. Strong after-sales support builds brand loyalty and repeat sales. Customers will buy the better-designed, better-supported products if they are similarly priced. Design advantages, coupled with a strong marketing and support programs, can enable companies to stay competitive over the long term.

The increasing allocation of resources to design and marketing is shown in Fig. 15.3.

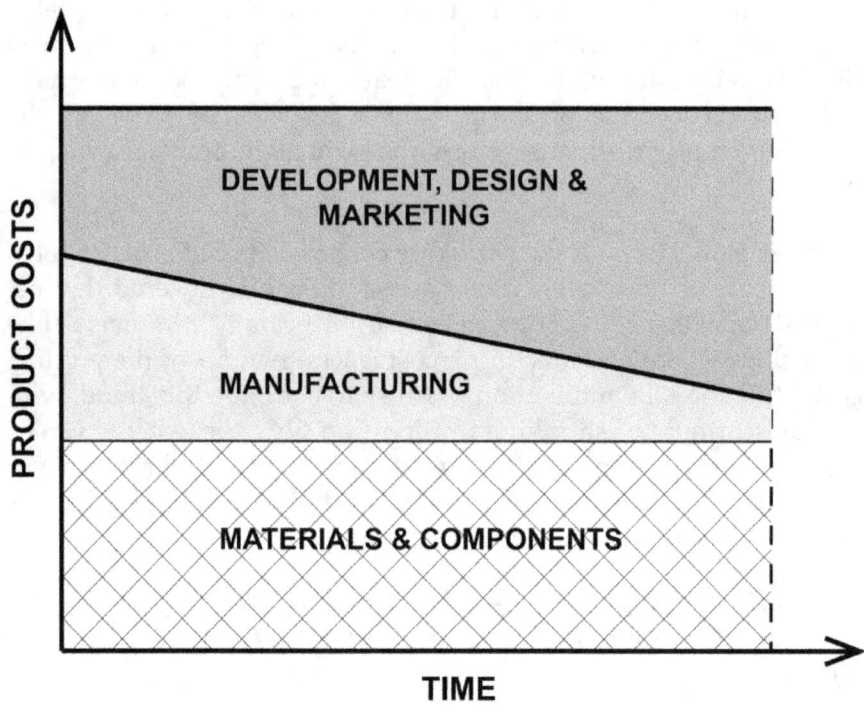

Figure 15.3 The evolution of product costs over time.

Advancements in *artificial intelligence* (**AI**) and *highspeed wireless communication* (**5G**, ...) technologies will further accelerate the demise of existing learning curves. Such developments will lead to major advances in user interfaces, self-driving vehicles, autonomous robots, etc. - changes that will radically change how people live and work.

Value of Forecasting

Some may question the value of forecasting the future given the many uncertainties. Analyzing trends to predict the future is equivalent to using available data for the forecasting. While there will always be uncertainties, such analyses reduce uncertainty in forecasts.

Since the goal of business is to "win" more than competitors, better forecasting is consistent with that goal. Such analyses are part of every manager's job, namely, to maximize successes now and in the future.

And What About Vision?

Management vision is the ability to envision and communicate future markets changes before they are well-supported by data. It is a subjective skill that separates many leaders. Strong intuition, creativity, and passion are hallmarks of visionaries. Visionary managers are more successful at formulating long-term strategies.

While a desirable trait, vision is not a skill every manager needs to personally possess. Vision can be brought into an organization by recruiting proven visionaries. The problem is who to recruit and whose vision to believe?

This is where objective analysis plays a role. While objective analysis cannot replace vision, it can be used to evaluate different visions to assess uncertainties (risks) and benefits (rewards) if they become true. All else being equal, it makes sense to choose ones with the greatest rewards for a given level of risk.

Fig. 15.4 below compares three different strategic visions. Strategy **B** offers the highest Reward/Risk, even though its potential rewards are lower than strategy **A**. Strategy **C** has almost the same Reward/Risk as **B**, but with lower risk and rewards. **B** would be the choice based on Reward/Risk alone, however, **C** might be preferable to minimize risks. The actual choice will depend on the goals of the organization, and the strategic importance of the particular program. For example, Strategy **A** might be appropriate if it is a "bet your company" situation in a hyper-competitive environment, since it offers the greatest rewards.

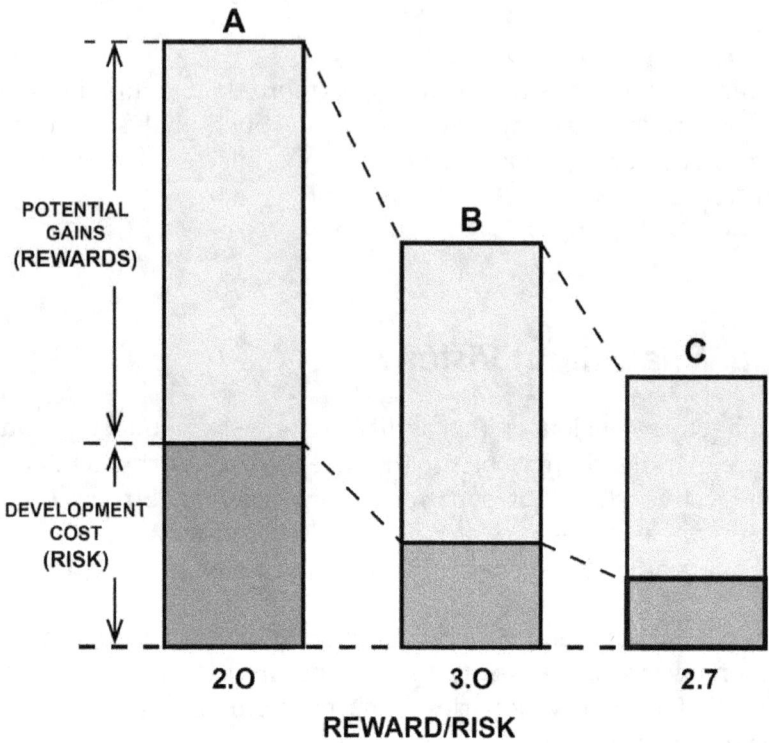

Figure 15.4 Comparing REWARD/RISK for three hypothetical strategic visions.

When strategies are based on a vision, objective analyses can serve as the framework for rationalizing the selection. Visions are easier to sell when they are supported by logic.

Some Steps for Monitoring Long-Term Needs

1. Have clear long-range goals

Identifying roadblocks is difficult if one does not know where one is going. Management vision needs to be combined with clear long-range goals - goals that are both competitive and achievable. Although there is always risk that one's goals are wrong, objective analyses using available information can minimize that risk.

2. Identify trends

Trends that alter future business environments need to be examined to assess whether current products and services will still be competitive in the future. If forecasts show they will not, new strategies and approaches need to be found.

3. Monitor trends

Unanticipated developments can alter trends. The further into the future the goals, the greater the likelihood of surprises. Consequently, environments need to be monitored to ensure underlying assumptions remain valid. If trends or assumptions change, the strategies need to be updated.

Summary

Long-term business success requires anticipating future changes in the market and allocating resources to respond to those changes. This requires monitoring trends and knowing when one's products and services are going to mature (i.e., reach learning curve saturation). The ability to forecast the future equal or better than competitors is key for business leadership.

Vision is a skill that enables some people to predict the future beyond what can be deduced from existing data. It is a skill that enables certain individuals to identify future markets before others. Objective analyses supplement such skills by providing tools for assessing different visions.

Closing Comments

In this book I have promoted a common-sense approach to management: learning as much as possible about a problem and using logical reasoning to formulate solutions that maximize chances for success. While some of the analytical approaches may seem time consuming, the procedures can become second nature with practice and saves time over the long term. The best part is their value increases with accumulated learning, so their effectiveness grows over time.

As I have said repeatedly in this book, the techniques are meant to supplement, not replace, intuitive skills like vision and passion. They can multiply such strengths and suppress unconstructive tendencies like prejudice, anger, and fear.

Fig. 15.5 is one last cartoon, comparing a leader who proceeds solely by intuition versus one who utilizes logical reasoning and available information.

"I have a good sense of direction. I think we should head in that direction.."

"Based on this map and our GPS position this path should get us to our destination."

Figure 15.5 Which guide would you follow?

www.ingramcontent.com/pod-product-compliance
Lightning Source LLC
Chambersburg PA
CBHW070338220526
45467CB00001B/161